Ga

Gayatri Sadhana

OM SWAMI

First published in India in 2018 by
Jaico Publishing House

Worldwide publishing rights: Black Lotus Press

ISBN: 978-9388423243

Contents

APPENDIX

Why This Book

I once read a beautiful story that really touched my heart.* A master and his disciple were seeking alms and they stopped by a small home. Whether the tiny size of the home was more worthy of one's notice or its dilapidated condition was anyone's guess.

"Praise the Lord!" the master hollered and knocked at the door. "We've come for alms." There was no response from anyone who might be inside that one-room house. "*Bheeksham dehi*," he said in a loud voice again and waited for another minute. No one came out. In line with their tradition, he made a third and final call. Soon, a little girl came running out.

"Sorry, master," she said, "but we have nothing to give you."

The monk looked at her lovingly and said, "Don't say no, my daughter. Can you give me a handful of dust from the ground?"

---

* I have paraphrased this story a bit but I first read it in *Kadve Pravachan* by Muni Tarun Sagar, the famous Jain monk.

"Dust?" she said, surprised.

"Yes, a handful will do."

Obliging the master, the girl bent down, took a bit of mud from the ground and put it in the master's bowl. He blessed her and walked away with his disciple. The disciple was both intrigued and upset. Intrigued because he thought his master's action was absurd, and upset for their tradition permitted alms from one house only on any given day. *Who eats dust? Will have to do with water today. My master's lost his mind or what?*

"Why, master?" he said, unable to control his curiosity. "What are we going to do with dust? We could have just visited the next home and gotten proper alms."

"My son," the master said, "by remaining hungry, today we have transformed one life."

The disciple couldn't make sense of this statement while the master continued speaking, "I introduced her to the joy and merit of charity. *Aaj dhool di hai, kal phool bhi degi.*" (Today she learned to give a handful of earth, one day, she'll give a flower too.)

So it is with sadhana, the path of elevating your life and others' by continuously purifying yourself. Today if you undertake a basic spiritual practice, overcome a small hurdle, tomorrow you'll be able to take on a more advanced one, handle bigger challenges. Since my last book on mantras, I have met over 1500 people in one-on-one meetings and more than 3000 in groups. A common issue, even complaint, is that what I wrote in that book is daunting, to say the least. Some of the steps were not clear, they said. That, it's very hard to muster the courage to undertake intense sadhana. That, if I could recommend just one sadhana, which one would it be. And finally, if I could give them a simpler method, something that appears more within reach, it would motivate them.

It made me think and like the monk in our story, I thought if I could introduce you to a simpler (read easier) way of sadhana today, then who knows, tomorrow you may feel confident and motivated to take on something more intense. After all, when you go to learn music from a teacher, not every student spends his time learning ragas, some just want to be able to sing or play simple songs and find joy in that.

I've written this book with the view that at least I should introduce you to the power, rewards and joy of sadhana. For instance, once you know how to play/sing a few songs, you may feel inclined to go deeper. In doing so, I am still expounding on the thirty-six core steps of sadhana as well as giving you the much shorter method of using only seven key steps. You can undertake whichever you like more based on your temperament, schedule and goals. Both ways are almost equally rewarding, one being more immersive than the other.

Thank you for trusting me; it is the basis of my inspiration and writings. As always, in this book too, I share with you the truth as I know it. Even for a moment I don't forget that my utmost duty is not to fascinate you with tall claims of something out there, something supernatural, but to share with you the miracle of what's inside us naturally. This discovery is just as beautiful, empowering and liberating.

Let's take a walk.

Why Gayatri Mantra

Where should I begin? Although I have chosen the path of meditation in my own life, much of what I know, if not all of it, is attributable to the grace of Divine Mother. In this day and age, when we are conditioned with Western thought, it is natural to question the efficacy or the relevance of mantras.

I can tell you from my first-hand experience that the power of mantras is one, immense, two, real, and three, accessible. When we listen to music, we can hear the harmony within it – and we know that certain chords, melodies, rhythms and scales can evoke certain emotions in us. This is regardless of whether we know how to sing, play an instrument or read music notation, etc.

As a listener, listening to music can make you cry, it can make you laugh and so on. Similarly – and it's not just a metaphor: it is very real – whether or not you know it, the sound of mantras can bring alive long-forgotten memories in you. Tendencies, feelings, emotions, knowledge, wisdom, powers and *siddhis** you have been carrying within yourself over lifetimes can be evoked and invoked with the power of a mantra.

The abiding dilemma in Sanatana Dharma is, what is that one supreme energy one should tap into? People ask me this all the time that there are so many gods or forms of God, to whom should we pray? Most fascinatingly, even in a religion as diverse as Sanatana Dharma, with as many sects as stars in the sky (okay, maybe not as many), there's one Vedic mantra that has been widely recognized as the quintessential mantra of our dharma.

Even though I'm calling Sanatana Dharma a religion – commonly known as Hinduism – it is actually not a religion but a way of life, a manner of thinking. Therefore, in India's ancient or medieval history, you will never find an episode of two kings or states going to battle just because they prayed to a different form of God. It is quite remarkable that in a country with tens of languages and hundreds of dialects, a country with extraordinary cultural and historical diversity, where states were eternally fighting territorial and political wars, there had never been any persecution in the name of religion. That's because Sanatana Dharma allowed peaceful co-existence of contradictions.

Wherever you might have been in this beautiful country, through any period in its several millennia-old history, Sanatana Dharma has stood on four pillars – *Gau*, cow; *Gita*, the *Bhagavad Gita*, which means the song of the Lord, and is our scripture; Ganga, Mother Ganga, and Gayatri.

---

* *Siddhis* are supernatural powers stated in various yogic and Puranic texts.

Adi Shankaracharya wrote in *Bhaja Govindam*, "*Gaiyam gita naam sahasram, dheyam shripati roopamajasram, neyam sajan sange chitam, deyam deen janaye chavittam.*"

The purpose of human life is fourfold. *Gaiyam gita naam sahasram;* Shankaracharya urges that whenever your mind has a moment to spare, chant the holy names, sing the divine glories and express your gratitude to the Divine. (It's better than gossiping, sulking or speaking ill of anyone.) Because, as you have heard in my earlier discourses, nothing gives you strength like gratitude, happiness and inner peace. Happiness is a direct outcome of your gratefulness. The more grateful you are, the happier you will feel.

Dheyam shripati roopamajasram: Meditate upon the divine energy. *Neyam sajan sange chitam*: Spend your time in the company of good people – it's the hardest thing to do.

When you socialize with other people, you will discover that they spend more of their time gossiping than doing anything else, and it goes beyond the standard exchanging of pleasantries: "Hey, how are you doing today?" It's just plain gossiping. This weakens you, because when you relax in your free time, your mind always plays back what it had heard during the day. That's how the mind works. If you don't feed it garbage, it won't feed you garbage back.

Shankaracharya said, "*Neyam sajan sange chittam.*" Spend your time in the company of good people. I once read somewhere that at any point in time, you will discover that you are a reflection of the five most significant people in your life. We become the kind of people we surround ourselves with. The whole premise of meditation, of *bhakti*, of devotion, is based on this alone – that if I have to derive my inspiration from somebody, let that person not be an ordinary person with ordinary challenges; with ordinary, petty thinking. Let me derive my inspiration from something grand, something extraordinary; something beautiful.

"Deyam deen janaye chavittam" means be charitable to those who are needy. Such a life is useless where you live just for yourself. Somewhere your life has to have meaning. It has to be of use to somebody else, to some other people, because the unfailing law of the universe is whatever you give, it will grow. With that in mind, share your resources with those who need it. So these four pillars of Sanatana Dharma form the basis of a meaningful life, of a purposeful life: So that we speak our words carefully, use our resources judiciously to help ourselves and those around us and be eternally grateful for everything in our lives.

This particular book is about the fourth pillar: the Gayatri mantra. My view is that by the time you finish this book, you will know, a) How to invoke the Gayatri mantra because until you invoke it, you won't benefit from it and b) Even more importantly, how to put it to use. Merely accumulating the energy of the mantra is not enough, one needs to know how to benefit from it. It's like having a million dollars in your bank account but not knowing how to withdraw the money; you don't have any cheque book or an ATM card.

Mantra science is something like that. The wealth that you seek, the spiritual wealth, is inside you. It's already there. The question is, how do you put it to use? Now, there are many methods and I don't want to give you more methods. (I did that extensively in my book *The Ancient Science of Mantras.*) Here, I want to make it extremely simple for you.

A wife was leaving home to go to the market.

She said to her husband, "Honey, I am going out for a couple of hours, do you need anything from the market?"

He smiled and said, "Thanks, that's enough!"

Chanting is a little like this. What I am going to share with you may seem like nothing at the end of the day, but depending on your state of mind, this is going to be enough. Notably, mantras, including the Gayatri mantra, have no creators. Mantras have what we call seers, which means rishis or sages who saw them first. So the wisdom is already there – we only need eyes to see it.

Of the four Vedas, Rig Veda is considered the oldest. In the Rig Veda, Third Canto, 61st Chapter, Mother Divine is referred to as Usha. Usha means dawn; Usha means daybreak, the first light. Mother Divine is referred to as the light. But it is in the 3rd Canto, 62nd Chapter and 10th Verse where the Gayatri mantra is first featured in any scripture.

The verses in Vedas are organized in meters, called *chanda* in Sanskrit, and Krishna says, "*Gayatri naam chandasaam aham*"* (The Bhagavad Gita 10.35). Here,

* The full verse is: *bṛihat-sāma tathā sāmnāṁ gāyatrī chhandasām aham māsānāṁ mārga-śhīrṣho 'ham ṛitūnāṁ kusumākaraḥ*. Thus: Of the Vedas, I'm Samaveda; of meters, I'm Gayatri; of months, I'm Margashirsha; and of seasons, I'm spring, Krishna says. This also hints at the esoteric aspect of Gayatri sadhana, that is, if one wishes to invoke the mantra of Gayatri for both material and spiritual upliftment, the month of *Margashirsha* (usually mid Nov–mid Dec, but please consult *panchangam*

Krishna says, of all the Vedic meters, I am Gayatri. The meter of Gayatri has many mantras, with Gayatri mantra being the most significant. In other words, the meter of the Gayatri mantra is also Gayatri. Under Gayatri *chanda*, the meter of Gayatri, the Gayatri mantra sits in the third canto, 62nd chapter, 10th verse, and it does not begin with the usual *Bhur-bhuvah-svah.* The mantra found there is:

Tat-savitur-varenayam
Bhargo-devasya-dhimahi
Dhiyo-yo-nah-prachodayat.

The complete and recommended mantra, however, begins with *Om bhur-bhuva-svaha.* To understand the structure, power and energy of the Gayatri mantra, we have to revisit a chapter in our ancient history, when, how and under what circumstances the first rishi invoked this mantra.

---

for the exact lunar dates) or the spring season is the best time to begin your *purushcharana.*

The First Practitioner

The valiant king Kaushika was returning with a large number of men – his troops and his entourage. They were tired and worn out from the long battle they had just won. Passing through the woods, they thought they should camp somewhere but, the trouble was, they had run out of provisions. And without food, even the greatest warriors can't survive, so the king was concerned. *How am I going to feed my people? My soldiers are weary now, I cannot let them starve.*

Just as this was going through his mind, one of his ministers said, "There is a small ashram in the woods, the hermitage of Sage Vasishtha. It's a small place; we will not be able to feed ourselves there, but perhaps we can drink some water and relax a little."

When they arrived at the ashram, King Kaushika prostrated before the sage who was said to be almost as old as the universe itself. The glow on his face, his flowing white beard, his snow-white matted locks on his medium-built body of wheatish complexion looked as if twilight meeting the morning sun. The king said with reverence, "We would just like to take a short rest here."

"You look rather tired," the rishi said, "and your men, exhausted. Rest here for as long as you like, I'll make meal arrangements for all of you."

"With due respect, O sage," the king said with a chuckle, "I don't think you can feed us all – there are many of us – my entire army is here."

"You underestimate the power of penance, O King," Vasishtha replied. "I am a rishi. I can feed and satiate the entire universe except for Brahma, Vishnu and Shiva, who are satiated on their own accord alone. The one who does not seek anything, the one who does not need anything from the world, can create anything he so wishes."

This is one of the greatest secrets of the universe: When you are fulfilled, you can manifest fairly much anything in your life. It's when we are not fulfilled that we become impatient; we become self-centered. We become tired and narrow-minded. In chasing what we could have had, we lose sight of what we already have.

"You sure? Because I would not want that a few of our men are fed and the others remain unfed. Besides," Kaushika said, "I don't see anything here: I don't see many pupils or disciples of yours. How are you going to cook such a massive meal?"

"Leave that to me," the rishi said. "Why don't you all go and take a dip in the river? By the time you get back, hot food will be ready." The king was now quite intrigued. Nevertheless, he did what he was told, so along with his men, they marched down to the river. Due to rains from the night before, the water was a bit muddy, yet they all bathed. *Let alone food, how will he give us even enough clean water to drink?* When they returned, they sat down for the meal, and one after the other, they were served – plates full of food along with glasses filled with crystal clear spring water.

"Eat to your heart's content," the sage said. "There is no dearth of anything here."

Now then, it was only natural that after he had eaten, Kaushika thought, how could he do this? A sage, on his own, feeding a king and his army? It's unheard of, quite incredible.

"How did you make this happen?" he asked Vasishtha.

"I have a cow, a female calf called Nandini, given to me by Indra, and Indra has a wish-fulfilling cow called Kamadhenu. Nandini is the calf of Kamadhenu, and she fulfills wishes."

He is a sage, an ascetic. What need does he have for a calf like that? What if I had it in my kingdom. I could feed everybody; I would become supreme. I could travel with my army with just one calf beside us, and she would feed us all. We would never run out of food. We could keep conquering territories after territories.

Kaushika got thinking. *This sage does not need all this power. It's something that should belong to a king.*

"So how does this work?" he asked Vasishtha. "This calf, can you request anything of her? Does she grant anything you ask? For instance, if I said, fill my treasury with gold, would she do it?"

"She can grant anything you need in the present moment," the sage said. He knew where this was going but he kept his calm. "Anything you may require in the future, she cannot, because that goes against the fabric of nature.

For nature never hoards; nature exists in the present, progressing from one moment to another. So Nandini only provides whatever you require now."

"That will also do. I ask you, please give me this calf."

"I'm sorry, Your Majesty, that cannot happen, because she has come here by grace, and she is treated like a mother. Besides, you are a king; you will use her solely for your material gains. I, however, have used her boons for the welfare of others: to feed hungry people."

Kaushika was unimpressed. The desire to possess Nandini had taken over, and the basic foundation of Sanatana Dharma – respect for your elders – was crumbling under the weight of ambition. "I am your king and you are in my kingdom, and I am the one who is supporting you. Therefore, I demand that you give me your calf."

"I seek your forgiveness but, I cannot. Nandini is under my care and protection. She is my gift, and she is Mother Divine to us."

"Protection?" Kaushika laughed loudly. "You, a lone, aging sage will protect her from *my* army? Give her to me." Saying this, he nodded to his chief minister.

Vasishtha kept quiet to indicate his disapproval.

"Well, I will take her then." The king moved a step in the direction of the calf. This was the beginning of their lifelong discord. "Don't say I didn't warn!"

"You cannot," Vasishtha replied with a chilling conviction and calm in his voice.

"How will you protect yourself?" Kaushika said. "Just take a look at my army. They are powerful like the ocean. They will overwhelm you in no time at all."

"You may not take Nandini."

While this ruckus was going on, Kaushika's men had untied Nandini from her post. Vasishtha immediately moved to the spot where Nandini was and she said to Vasishtha, "Why are you are giving me away? What wish of yours have I not fulfilled? I like it here in the woods. This is my place. I don't want to go from here."

"I am not giving you away, O mother," Vasishtha said. 'He is taking you and he is testing me. But you are the mother, and I am your child. I will use the power of my penance but it is with your grace alone. Bless me."

Vasishtha whispered a mantra and used a *kriya* called *stambhan* in Tantra. *Stambhan* is the method of making anything stop. You can do *agni-stambhan*, for example, which stops fire, *jala-* or *vayu-stambhan* to stop rain or air, and so on. Vasishtha stopped Kaushika's army. His men were rooted to the spot; they could not move even an inch. Soon, their bodies became unbearably heavy, their joints hurt and extreme depression seeped into their heads. They became suicidal. Several hours passed after which the king apologized and pleaded with Vasishtha to forgive and release him and his army.

Kaushika returned to his palace with the fire of revenge burning his heart, that whisper of a mantra seething his ears. "I was ridiculed and had to beg for forgiveness in front of my own men. I, Kaushika, got defeated by somebody who didn't even carry a weapon. This is not befitting of my status. I need the power this sage has. In the woods, he is fulfilled. He can manifest anything, and he is protected. I am no longer going to conquer territories and rule. I'm going to attain the power of this sage." With that, he decided to renounce his kingdom and devote his life to *tapas.*

Tapas is penance, not in the form of just repentance, but in the form of invocation. With all his fervor, Kaushika prayed to Shiva for 1000 years, the original creator of mantras.

"*Varam bhoohi*," Shiva appeared in his glorious form and said. Ask for a boon.

"I would like the finest weapons, the kind of which that if I used them on anybody, they would stand no chance of survival."

Shiva granted his request and gave him many weapons, *astras* – arms that he could dislodge like divine shafts, arrows, sonic missiles – and *shastras* – the ones he could carry with himself like an impenetrable shield, an unbreakable sword and many others.

Drunk on his revenge still as new as his newly-found powers, he headed straight to Vasishtha's ashram and roared, "Where are you hiding?" The sun rays sparkling against the shiny, razor-sharp sword he held aloft made him look like an indomitable warrior.

Vasishtha came out of his hermitage, and said, "How can I serve you?"

"Drop all these false niceties, you old fool! Give me Nandini or get ready for a battle! Reject my instruction and I am going to utterly destroy you, this very moment."

Vasishtha said calmly, his beard flowing in the gentle breeze, "Please, it's not necessary. I cannot give you Nandini."

'Then be prepared to die," Kaushika said, "No one can stop me from taking Nandini today!"

"Try," was the only word the sage uttered in reply.

One after the other Kaushika unleashed his weapons on Vasishtha. Vasishtha took out his staff – the rishi used to carry a *Brahma danda* or staff – and he held it in front of him. The energy of the weapons Kaushika launched at him was absorbed by the staff. Once Kaushika's weapons were spent, Vasishtha simply tilted his staff a little, casting a massive orb of energy at him. Kaushika fell down, defeated. "You are my guest," Vasishtha said. "I will not hurt you anymore. Please leave. Do something better with yourself, and don't ask for Nandini again."

Kaushika was foaming at his mouth, his face red like raging fire.

I've spent 1000 years on this, and I can't even get a cow! Shiva's weapons couldn't help me at all, he thought. He decided he would pray to Shiva no more. With that, he began invoking Hiranyagarbha, the golden womb, the first cell in creation. *I must go to the absolute source of this existence*, he decided. One thousand years later, Brahma appeared and granted him his Brahmastra, his most potent weapon. "Take this," he said. "If there is anything another weapon can do, this weapon can do it better."

Once again, Kaushika confronted Vasishtha but unfortunately, he met the same fate. Finally, the king accepted his defeat and accepted the fact that he couldn't win over Vasishtha. And then a realization dawned on him when Vasishtha told him the secret.

"It's not my power, O king," the sage said, "It is but who I am. You are not defined by what you have or what you can do, but by who you are, deep inside you."

"You have been doing all this penance to attain something, but you have forgotten your own attainment: you have not invoked the divinity in you," he continued. "You are simply carrying some *siddhis*, supernatural powers, to further your cause. You are not tapping into your real source of power, so you can have all the weapons in the world, but still won't match me, because for me, my strength is not in this staff," he said, throwing it away. "It's in but who I am."

Hearing this, Kaushika thought: *No more am I going to seek weapons or harbor animosity. Instead, I will aim to reach the same level of consciousness, rather superconsciousness, like Vasishtha to whom even Indra bows down and the powers of the universe look up to.*

Quietly he took Vasishtha's leave and sat in searing penance lasting several thousand years. Wishing welfare of all sentient beings, with awakened self and heightened consciousness, he saw the most mystical of all mantras, the one that dispels ignorance. It was clear to Kaushika that enlightenment alone was the answer to everything he sought. From a king eager to conquer territories, he became a sage who ruled hearts. So much so that he was given the title 'Vishwamitra' – a friend of the whole world.

But, detached from the world, Vishwamitra wasn't interested in any titles. After all, he had been an emperor once. Instead, his heart was set on the most supreme knowledge, something that would not only make him another Vasishtha but even better. *So what if I wasn't born a Brahmin?* he thought. He could, with his penance, not only purify himself so much that he would be a Brahmin but go even beyond. And beyond he went. With his unrelenting and intense *tapas*, one by one, *siddhis* and greater powers came to him. And he absorbed all of it like a giant tree absorbs nutrients from the earth and light from the sun. Vishwamitra acquired such a towering stature that he was regarded as 'Brahmarishi' – a Brahmin sage, the highest honor any sage could have.

With his inner eye, he had seen the one mantra, the essence of the Vedas, the cause of creation, the one mantra that had the power to pull anyone out of any adversity, that congregation of divine sounds which could help one realize one's wildest dreams. The only mantra he ever invoked ever since he left Vasishtha's ashram – the Gayatri mantra.

The door is wide open, your portal to another dimension of consciousness begins by understanding the power, invocation and realization of the metascience of the Gayatri mantra. As long as you are in this body made up of five elements, you can benefit from this mantra in much the same manner as Vishwamitra and numerous other sages did. In fact, the good news is that since the Gayatri mantra has already been invoked, you and I don't have to put in the same effort. Someone has already dug the well, you just have to lower the bucket to fill it. At least, that's been my personal experience in this lifetime.

Let me show how to go about invoking the Gayatri mantra in this day and age in simple and actionable steps. Even if you are not convinced, I only have one thing to say: what harm is there in trying? Besides, you won't know what all awaits you until you make the first move.

The Power of Gayatri Mantra

There are many forms of Gayatri, but one particular form is called Savitur Gayatri, which is derived from the word Savitri, the name of Mother Divine, radiant and effulgent. Bear in mind that while Mother Divine, like our solar system, engenders light, until we invoke the light within, the world around us is dark. And there is little hope for the person who remains dark inside.

The Vedas talk about four states of mind: *sushupta*, when you are sleeping; *jagrita*, when you are awake; *swapana,* when you are dreaming, and *turiya,* when you are beyond. There are also seven planes of existence, of which three are key: *bhu*, this material plane; *bhuvah*, the plane of consciousness and *svah*, our true self, something that is even beyond consciousness. The experience you might go through when you are unconscious is an experience that is beyond consciousness.

Consciousness itself is vital for mantra sadhana. It is essential to remember with chanting any mantra, and certainly the Gayatri mantra, that it's not about becoming a parrot and keep chanting without any feeling. Some people just want to get through the mantra as if it's a task they have taken upon themselves: "Good lord, do I want to sit and chant this mantra again? As if I don't have enough to do in my life, and I have taken upon myself one more thing?"

If you are going to chant the mantra with this sentiment, you will not get any results from it – you may understand, but not benefit from the mantra. This is the most important, qualitative aspect of mantra science, and it simply cannot be ignored. In that sense, it's not a traditional science – it requires faith.

Another important aspect of mantra science is learning its proper use. When you chant mantras, and when the grace of Mother Divine is fully bestowed upon you, you will realize when and how to use it. That discretion, that sense of discerning wisdom, comes after a long time of mantra sadhana.

Initially when you gain power and sharpened intuition, or when you feel you can bless somebody and make a difference to somebody's life, you will be tempted to say, "Yes, granted, okay, so be it," because you want to make others happy. Or worse, you may simply want to impress people. But let's assume your intention is simply to make others happy. To say, "Oh, this person is bothered by this, let me make him happy." Or you'll say, "Oh, granted, you'll win a million dollars tomorrow," and so on. If you do that, you will lose the power very quickly indeed – in a matter of weeks, or even days, if you're not lucky. There is a saying in Hindi, *Bandar ke haath ustra lag gaya hai.* The monkey's got a razor in his hands and it's now just running it over everything it sees.

That's why when you chant a mantra, it takes time for the energy to come to you: Nature is preparing you so you are ready to provide a real benefit to society.

People will come to you, and only one percent of them will come simply to say, "I am very happy, I just wanted to express my gratitude." Ninety-nine percent of people will come to you with problems, almost all of whom would believe they are not the cause of them. If someone believes he is not the cause of his problem, how can we solve it? If he believes that something else is causing the issue, and says, "Fix the problem, but don't tell me to do anything, because I am not the cause of it," you might say, "Okay, your problem will be solved."

There was this person in Canada – and I am telling you his real-life story, which I witnessed over a period of time. When I first met him in India, he was a devout worshipper of the Gayatri mantra. He was the first one whom I saw who actually had Gayatri *siddhi*. *Siddhi* is when a mantra becomes your own and you become the mantra; the energy of the mantra works through you, lives in you, benefitting other people. He blessed and helped many people sail through difficult circumstances in life.

When I first met him, this man's radiance was extraordinary. He had such a beautiful, effulgent face; you could look at him all day, and still feel as if you were receiving the love, warmth, divinity and grace that flowed from him. Those were the days when I did a lot of astrology – I was 15 years old then.

This *sadhaka's* dedication was phenomenal. He had been chanting the Gayatri mantra, 16 rounds, every day. One round of chanting is 108 times. Every day for roughly 40 years, he never missed his chanting routine.

I'll digress for a moment to tell you a little incident from his life. The factory where he used to work got a big order once, so they asked everybody to put in half a shift more each day. That way, two people could do 12 hours' work each in different shifts, so the factory could have 24 hours of production. This was back in the early nineties.

He said to his boss, "Look, I am sorry, I cannot stay back, because at 3 pm I have to leave. I have to do my own thing then – it's my personal time."

"You have been with this company for 20 years," his boss said. "You know how big this order is for us. And it's not as if we're not paying you. We will pay you double the usual amount for the overtime. All we are asking is that you extend your work day for four hours, and only for eight or nine weeks."

He said, "Sorry, I can't do that."

"That's not going to sit well with anybody. You're the supervisor. What kind of example are you going to set?"

"I'm sorry, I need to put food on the table, but I cannot stay beyond 3 pm."

The manager became quite upset. The matter went to the department head, and he had a meeting. He said the same thing and then it went all the way to the CEO. Because he had been working at the factory for 20 years, they couldn't just fire him. They needed people with the technical know-how who could fulfill the order.

"I'm at my wits' end," the CEO said. "Why do you *have* to go at 3 pm? Why can't you stay back for four hours, just for a few weeks? Tell me, what is the problem? Won't you be happy if this company grows?"

"It's a personal thing," he replied. "I have to go and meet somebody."

"You don't exactly look like a teenager in love. Whom do you have to meet every day that you can't miss? Can't you meet him or her at 7 pm?"

"I must reach home by 4 pm, when I sit down and have my meeting."

"But with whom?" the CEO asked, a bit flustered. 'Whom do you have to meet?"

I am not adding any of my own words. This is exactly how I heard this from the man himself.

"Well, I have to meet the person who gave me this job," he said.

"This is the craziest thing I've ever heard," the CEO said, throwing his hands in the air. "What are you talking about? I gave you this job. This is my damn company!" Then the CEO thought, perhaps there was some agent involved. This guy is a poor immigrant, so there must have been an agent who is taking a commission or some work from the employee that he is unaware of.

So he said, "Oh I get it! Is there some kind of agent in between us? But, I gave you this job myself."

"No, there's no agent, but I can tell you whom I must meet at 4 pm every day."

"Pray tell," the CEO said, exasperated.

"Do you know Jesus?" this man asked.

"If you mean Jesus Christ, then of course, I know him."

"Well, I go home to meet his father. I pray to Krishna."

For 40 years this person had never missed his routine of Gayatri mantra chanting. Every day, he chanted 16 rounds of the mantra and two rounds of Hare Krishna Mahamantra, followed by reading one chapter from the *Bhagavad Gita.* He was a householder and worked a full-time job until he was 60 years old. This is the level of self-discipline and faith that is required if you really want to succeed on the path of mantra sadhana.

The CEO, for the record, marked on his file to never to bother this guy again: Let him do whatever he wants to do after 3 pm; let him go where he wants to go, in his own time. He worked till he retired from this company, by the way. Look at his faith. So often, we think that people who are just mediums in our lives are our everything, that without their grace we won't live. That's not true. They are simply the medium. '*Ja par kripa raam ki hoi, taa par kripa kare sab koi.*' (If the Divine is in your favor, the whole world will be too.)

A very senior bureaucrat once wrote to me, saying, "The chief minister used to love me, but now the CM is against me, and I am being framed," and so forth. He was very keen that I get his email, so I wrote him one line in return.

I wrote, "Did you do anything wrong?"

He replied, "No."

Then I wrote back to him, "You don't have anything to worry about. Drop all your fears." He wrote to me again a few days later.

He said, "It's miraculous! I don't know how it happened, but just yesterday evening, I managed to meet the cabinet secretary and the principal secretary. Everybody is on my side, and people who were against me are now saying that I was actually doing the right thing. But I just need to be back in the good books of the chief minister, because he's the man, after all."

Then I wrote back to him, "You have missed the point completely. The chief minister is not the maker of your destiny; he is just the medium. You just focus on doing the right thing, and the right things will follow automatically."

It's worth remembering here that when your faith is strong, no adversity in life can shake you. Otherwise, every little incident becomes a huge episode. Each minor hurdle, every small challenge looks like a mountain to climb, which it isn't. You have made it into a mountain, but it is nothing. Keep doing what you have to do, and you will make your own way.

In any event, when we chant a mantra such as the Gayatri mantra, we are not asking any supernatural being to help us. Instead, we are invoking our own latent energy; we are invoking the power within us. Associating it with a deity of some kind is a matter of meditation; of better focus, visualization and manifestation.

Anyway, I was telling you about this *sadhaka* in Canada who devoutly meditated on Gayatri. He told me some of the things he was doing for people to help them. Many people began approaching him to fulfill their material objectives.

"Don't you think," I said to him, "that using the power

of Gayatri mantra only to fulfill material desires is misusing it? Today you will make somebody happy, but tomorrow they will come to you with another problem, followed by another and another."

"I am using the energy while it's working for me," he said.

"Well, if there was a way to make somebody happy eternally, we would gladly do that, but this doesn't exist," I said to him, "using a mantra in this manner is like making a toilet brush out of a large inheritance of gold."

Now fast forward seven years, when I saw him again, I could not even recognize him. He looked like a mango that had been sucked dry and cast aside. He had lost his radiance and spiritual potency. The power in his voice had diminished noticeably, the charisma had disappeared. It was as if Mother Gayatri had decided, "I don't want to live in you anymore."

I spoke with him, and we talked about what had come about. We had known each other for years and he believed in me a great deal because one, many a time in the past I'd done his astrological charts and two, I was a practitioner of mantras myself. Many a time, we even compared our sadhana notes.

"How can I regain my lost power?" he asked me.

"Stop meeting people," I told him. "And if you cannot stop seeing people, then don't just say to them that Mother Divine would grant their wish, instead simply pray to Mother to do whatever is right for them. Because fulfilling their desires is not helping people. They don't know what's right for them, do they?"

Consider this for a moment: do we always know what we really want? And when we get it, are we ever any happier? Usually not. After a short time, we are back to feeling the way we felt before.

So this *sadhaka* completely stopped granting people's wishes, and believe it or not, in another 14 years, he started looking radiant again. But he no longer blesses people the way he used to.

It is the duty of every *sadhaka* to bless, though, because we don't earn everything for ourselves. We are not performing a mantra just to benefit ourselves – that's a very limited view. Of course, we have to help others, but we need to know how to help. We cannot say, "Okay, nothing bad will happen to you." Or, at least, we should very rarely say that. I say that to less than 0.05 percent of the people I meet.

Mostly, what comes from me is this: Mother Divine, you know what's going on, and you know everything, so you decide – you decide what your grace is. This person is thinking, if I have my way, that is grace, but usually, this is not the case.

In fact, a good prayer would be, "God, please don't listen to me. I think I am very smart, I think I've got it all figured out, but that's really not the truth. So please, if you will, don't listen to me." I think this is the greatest prayer. You can't go wrong then.

At any rate, after what he went through, this sadhaka changed his prayer to, "Oh God! Oh Mother, please live in my mind, live in my consciousness, then I will not feel anything negative." That means I will not think anything negative; I will not contemplate anything negative – therefore, I won't do anything negative. If I don't do anything negative, I won't have to suffer anything adverse. It is as simple as that. This is a much better, more beneficial prayer in my view.

Getting back to the Gayatri mantra, the reason I have taken the time to give you a background of the mantra and mantra science is because by following a certain discipline, day in, day out, some of you – maybe 5 or 10 percent of you – are actually going to achieve success with the mantra. You will then be able to help yourself and others. If, at that time, you already understand what you have tapped into, and know the power of what you have, you will use it wisely and judiciously.

Gayatri mantra is considered the seed of all Vedic mantras in the sense that on the path of mantra yoga, no mantra can be invoked until we first perform the invocation of Vedmata Gayatri, which is done by chanting the Gayatri mantra a night prior to starting any *purushcharana*. It is the method of seeking her permission. Savitur or Savitri, the presiding deity of the Gayatri mantra, is called '*Vedmata*', the Mother of all Vedas.

The structure of this mantra is referred to as *Chatushpadi*: *chatush* means four and *padi* means limbs, which corresponds to the four Vedas and four pauses in the mantra. Of the four pauses in the Gayatri mantra, the one in the Vedas starts with "*Tat-savitur-varenyama bhargo...*" But the sages of yore invoked it with the three prefixes of *bhu, bhuvah, svah.* So the complete mantra becomes:

"Om Bhurbhuvah Svah," first pause,
"Tatsaviturvarenyama," second pause,
"Bhargo Devasya Dhimahi," third pause,
"Dhiyo Yo Nah, Pracodayata," fourth pause.

Bhur-bhuvah Svah are three planes of existence, three types of consciousness, three modes of material nature: *sattva, rajas* and *tamas* – the modes of goodness, passion and ignorance. *Tat* is that, *savitur* means something that's radiant; it is also the name of the sun, and radiant, divine energy. *Varenyam* is something that is of the colour saffron, or something that is fit to be worshipped.

There are all kinds of energies which may be invoked from all kinds of prayers or mantras, but not every deity is fit to be worshipped. You are going to derive your strength, inspiration, energy and radiance from your object of faith; from whomever you invest your faith in.

You see many tantrics, for example, who start to look like the deities they worship. I have heard that after many years of marriage, husbands and wives begin to look like brother and sister. The similarities become so pronounced that they even start to sound the same.

Bhargo means radiant, effulgent; *devasya* is divine; *dhimahi* is to meditate upon. *Dhiyo* means intellect; *yo* means which; *na* means our, and *pracodayata* is to put in motion. This mantra means we are now meditating upon the one who alone is fit to be worshipped. May that divine radiance, that divine energy which is full of light, guide our intellects. May it put our intellects in motion, so we have a certain wealth of wisdom to put to use. This is the basis of the Gayatri mantra.

In the beginning, when you chant this mantra, you follow a strict discipline, so to speak. You might only sit down and then chant. But as you progress, chanting becomes a part of your life, and you can chant 24/7.

Four Stages of Sound

If you have ever attended any of my meditation camps or discourses in person, then you must know that I always begin them with a short invocation and by offering my obeisance to the divine in you. I then quietly whisper, *Narayani Namostute*, which means that I bow down to that divine energy. I thought rather than offering you information on various stages of attainment based on age-old texts, I may as well offer you my own perspective, in my voice, based on my own experience in the present age.

When I say that I offer my obeisance to the divine in you, I actually mean it. It's not simply a matter of making a statement for me. It's a profound expression of how I feel about each living entity that I encounter. When you continually meditate on Divine Mother, you start to see her in everything. You see her in everybody, and people – their faces, bodies, colors and features – simply disappear. The first thing that comes in front of you is the form of Devi.

The first layer is Devi, Goddess, Energy, Divinity, whatever name you want to give, and the second layer is light. I see everybody as a light. Then the light disappears, and the third layer that I see is the actual human body. It wasn't like this before; it's not that it has been like this since I was born. This experience came about after my intense sadhana in the Himalayas. And the presence of the divine energy of Mother Divine is so real in my life that I really hope by the time you finish this book, that you would walk away with enough inspiration, as well as learning, to manifest the same in your life.

When that happens, the conflict between you and others will lessen drastically. You begin to flow gently with life. This does not mean you become weak – you remain strong; you know when to be firm and when to be soft. But you no longer use words to hurt others. When your speech becomes pure, with a pure heart and a pure mind, you become an embodiment of purity. Purity and light are synonyms of enlightenment, of freedom; while the impure is trapped and confined, the pure is eternally liberated.

Ultimately, the whole sadhana of Gayatri is to purify yourself. Otherwise, chanting has little meaning at the end of the day. If we fail to purify ourselves internally, then no mantra will ever yield any *siddhis* or powers. And *siddhis* will come to you, simply if you are purified.

Sometimes, people ask me, "Do you read minds?" or "How do you know who I am or my past, present or future?" You know, it's not that I sat down and chanted any specific mantra to invoke that kind of energy in me. Although there are some sadhanas that claim to do that, I never did them.

For example, there is a sadhana of a pishachini called karna pischani. Karna is your ear and pischini is a lower form of energy. It is said that Devi speaks in your ear. It's a tantric sadhana of the left-handed path.

My guru Naga Baba, who was a great tantric, once picked up his cell phone and said, "Beta, this is *karana pishachini. Yeh karana pishachani* hai, she is next to your ear and tells you everything." He was referring to his phone. This is the uber-connected lifestyle we have in this day and age. Anyway, it's not that I did any sadhana for that – it just happened naturally.

Through performing the mantra properly, a good meditator, a *sadhaka*, will naturally start to see through people, because the layers of various entities are peeled away. Then, you are not listening to people's words; you don't have to see their intentions; you are not looking at their bodies. Instead, you are connected on a different level altogether and when you are connected, you and that person are one at that point in time. You feel what that other person is feeling; you see what the other person is saying, and you recall what the other person knows. This connection is what truly differentiates an ordinary person from somebody purified; somebody who has really walked the path of the light, or in other words, this is the difference between an aspirant and adept.

For this level of spiritual attainment, you can never ignore the quality of our sadhanas. It's just as important for your wellbeing. What is the sense in chanting mantras, when you feel increasingly restless in your mind; when you feel just as angry, hurt, jealous and negative as you felt before you undertook any sadhana? Never overlook or underestimate the importance of purifying yourself. Otherwise, we are just being parrots when we chant.

A man went to a pet shop, where there was a parrot in a cage, constantly chanting, "Freedom, freedom, freedom, freedom, freedom."

The man said to the shopkeeper, "Does it only know one word?"

"No," the shopkeeper replied, "this parrot knows one more word," and the parrot started chanting, "Liberation, liberation, liberation."

"That's an enlightened parrot; I'd like to buy it." And so he bought the parrot and took it home.

All day, the parrot kept chanting, "Freedom, freedom, freedom, freedom," and the man's wife said, "Why don't you set this poor bird free? It will thank you." The man thought, *this is a kind gesture; I can certainly do this much.* So, he opened the cage door, and said, "Okay birdie, the door is open. Off you go, fly away, my fine feathered friend." But the parrot stayed on its perch and kept chanting, "Freedom, freedom, freedom," because it never understood what freedom was.

Chanting a mantra without awareness is like chanting "Food, food, food," and expecting your hunger to be satisfied – as if you could say, "*shahi paneer*", "dosa", "idli" or "pasta", and not need to feed yourself. If you reduce a mantra to a verbal activity, chanting recklessly just to finish the rounds, it won't take you anywhere.

There are four kinds of chanting, which lead to four progressive stages of sound. The first kind of chanting is called *vachika*, which means audible, verbal; something you speak. In *vachika*, Gayatri *japa* would be you chanting out loud, others around you can hear you easily. It is the most base level of *japa*. It will quickly tire you, and create restlessness in the mind if done over a prolonged period of time.

The second type of *japa* is called *upanshu* – your lips move, and you make only a whispering sound. It is like talking when you don't want to be heard. Two people in love, when close to each other, often whisper than talk out loud.

Sometimes, my mother's friends used to come home and talk like this. We would be sitting almost next to them and not know what they were saying. So it is with *upanshu*: only somebody who is no more than a few feet away from you can hear you. *Upanshu japa* is more effective than *vachika*.

The third kind of chanting is called *mansika* where you recall the whole mantra in your mind. There is no way I can demonstrate that. Usually, the mind keeps on talking, so rather than letting the mind ramble on, saying whatever it wants, *mansika japa* is making the mind say the particular mantra you are chanting.

Please note that *mansika japa* is not simply chanting the mantra in your mind, because that would simply be your mind chattering away. Instead, it is recalling the mantra in your mind – recollecting the mantra. In one moment you can only recall one thing. When you are simply chanting, speaking in your mind, part of your mind is elsewhere. Your mind is saying, *Om bhur-bhuvah svah tatsavitur-varenayama bhargo devasya dhimahi,* but you are thinking, *I have to make that phone call, I have to reply to that email; this person is waiting for me. That person wronged me, and I am not going to spare him; I'm just going to get on the phone and tell him what I think.*

If the mind is talking but only one aspect of the mind is chanting, that chanting is as good as useless. A more effective way of chanting is gentle and conscious recollection of your mantra. Picture a tap that's dripping, one drop after the other. Imagine that you are recalling in your mind the mantra between drips, that each section of the mantra is falling from the crown of your head one drop at a time: *Om bhur-bhuvah svah,* drip, *tatsavitur-varenayama,* drip, *bhargo devasya dhimahi,* drip, *dhiyo yo nah pracodayata,* drip. When you are recalling the mantra this way, your mind will concentrate better and your other thoughts will not intrude. It's a very subtle technique that I have figured out after years of practice and it has made a tremendous difference to the outcome I have gained from mantras.

For years I practiced mantra chanting without any significant results but the day I figured out how chanting was done properly, the impact of it changed. I began to notice some of the blessings that the scriptures promised.

It was not complete though, and to devote myself fully to my path of *tapas*, I left everything behind and went to the caves and woods. There, I devoted my time to invoking a mantra in the sense that the Devi, the deity of the mantra would come in front of me and talk to me. That's one of the ultimate achievements a *mantrin* – somebody who practices a mantra is called a *mantrin* – can attain.

The fourth *japa*, the ultimate one, is called *ajapa*. If you add 'a' in front of *japa*, it means the opposite of *japa*. Therefore, *ajapa* means you are not actually chanting – the mantra is chanting itself. With practice, you will get a grip over this. Some people will understand it in a matter of hours, for some it may be days, while for others it could be weeks. But if you stay on course, you'll understand what I am trying to say here.

While in the woods, I used to sit for very long hours – one straight stretch of ten hours, and then get up and do another stretch of six hours, and so on. It was very tiring: I would just sit like this and mentally chant (read recall) my mantra. At the end of every session, I would mark myself. And if during the ten hours I turned my head because there were rats and other creatures there distracting me, I would immediately deduct five marks out of ten, because my goal was to sit still like a rock, unmoving.

Sometimes, when I would cry out for Devi in devotion, it would actually interrupt my meditation, because tears would roll down my cheeks. It was icy cold, and when the tears emerged they were warm, but by the time they rolled down my cheeks, they were cold and my body consciousness rose.

When you sit still for long hours with extraordinary stillness and supreme concentration, you lose awareness of your body for a sustained period of time. You are sitting, you are mentally aware, but the body is not there anymore. This is not something I experienced on a daily basis, but this would happen often during long periods of meditation. For this, I would do a breathing technique and sometimes lose consciousness. In the beginning, when I would lose consciousness, I used to fall. There was a little wooden plank on the wall. The wall was also made of wooden planks, and my head would hit against the plank when I fell, and then I would come back to consciousness.

Sometimes my immersion in my *japa* was so intense, that while doing that breathing, I would hit my head against the wall and then return to consciousness after a minute or two. I knew the exact time, because I had a digital clock, so I would always know how I was doing against time if I were to keep my eyes open.

The most beautiful thing was that returning to consciousness was not like the flick of a switch. It was more like the coming of the dawn, so it would happen over a minute or so, and the first thing that would happen was, I would hear distant sounds such as people talking – sometimes, people talking about me. At that time, few people knew me – perhaps only a few hundred. Of those, 10 or 15 people may have been talking. There was not a day when my mother and my siblings did not think about me.

Sometimes, at the time I returned to consciousness, I would hear those distant conversations. Then, as I would regain my consciousness, I would only hear the mantra. Was the mantra going on when I was unconscious? I don't know. But this happened unfailingly when I did that breathing technique. Through this, I understood what *ajapa* actually entails: The moment you are in your consciousness, your mantra is chanting constantly within a part of you. So *ajapa* is not something you can do – *ajapa* is something that happens to you.

This is much like meditation. In the beginning, you do meditation, but as you progress, meditation happens to you. *Ajapa* is the ultimate state for a *mantrin* in terms of elevating your practice and taking it to the ultimate level. But you have to become one with the mantra, such that you may become the mantra itself; nothing but a vibration of the mantra. Every pore of your existence starts to reverberate with the sound of your mantra.

When you do *japa* in these four stages, it gives birth to four kinds of sounds. The first type of sound is *vaikhari. Vaikhari* is something that is produced artificially, by a person. When I am speaking, my tongue is touching my teeth or my palette and is producing some sound – that is *vaikhari*. Nature cannot produce this sound. Somebody, some element or entity in the play of nature creates the sound.

The second is *madhyama. Madhyama* is a sound that comes about by human intervention, but not created entirely by a person. Examples of *madhyama* could be the sound of someone slapping a tree or his thigh. With this clapping sound, I have not spoken anything.

The third is *pashyanti*, where absolutely no human intervention gives rise to the sound. The rustling of leaves is a good example of this. *Pashyanti* means the one that can be seen, or that which witnesses. You can see the fluttering of leaves and you can also hear the rustling sound they make.

The fourth sound is *para*, which means the one that is beyond, or absolute. When you do *ajapa* or when you do the *japa* and this kind of chanting happens to you – and even in the third kind, *mansika japa* – you start to move towards *para*, one of the finer states of consciousness.

I will give you a little analogy, which demonstrates what I mean by consciousness. Picture a very still lake –

there is not a sound, there is not a breath of wind, it is very quiet. On the bed of the lake, a tiny bubble forms. It's barely visible when it is at the bottom, but as it rises through the water, it becomes progressively bigger, and when it emerges, it's a huge bubble and makes ripples across the lake's surface.

Something similar happens with your consciousness when it is not under your control. Like tiny bubbles, thoughts or emotions come from the depths of your mind. As they rise within you, you feel increasingly out of control and they bubble to the surface, causing you disturbance. But if your consciousness is truly calm, no thoughts or emotions will form in the first place.

Physical chanting creates its own, small disturbances. When you do *vachika japa*, the first kind of *japa* where you do *vaikhari* sound, it's like tiny bubbles popping at the surface, because you are producing that sound. With the second kind, *madhyama*, the bubbles only form, but don't rise. While performing *mansika japa*, the bubbles actually travel to the surface. With the fourth, the *para* – while performing *ajapa* – no bubbles form in the water.

That stillness of the mind is the first requirement for experiencing the Divine in its truest sense, which is when you want to experience the divine energy – not just want to use it for your or others' benefit, but for its own sake.

For this, the mind has to be still, like that lake. With no bubbles in that stillness, you experience extraordinary bliss and crystal-clear awareness. When you chant in such pristine awareness, every word you utter will have a tremendous impact on your consciousness. There is only one way to gain that state, and that is practice – there is no other way that I know of.

Without practice, you may have intermittent or occasional experiences, but ultimately, these mean little. They don't mean that you are progressing unless you manifest a purity within you; unless you find yourself less angry at the world; unless you find yourself softer, mellower and more compassionate. Because a true spiritual experience is always transformational. If it hasn't transformed you, it is not a true experience – at least in the spiritual sense.

A disciple once asked his guru, "How do I gauge my spiritual progress? I have been chanting, I have been doing everything you have been telling me, but how do I know if I am progressing?"

The master said, "Just write down how many times you get disturbed in a day, and how many times you get upset over little things."

If you get upset very quickly, that means you are not progressing spiritually. If earlier you would get upset ten times in a day and now you only get upset five times a day, you are definitely progressing, because ultimately your spiritual progress must show through.

If you say to yourself, "Oh, I have done 1,00,000 *japa*," it really means nothing, it's like playing a tape – that parrot-tape.

A doctor had two parrots that were always chanting: *Hare Krishna Hare Krishna, Krishna Krishna Hare Hare, Hare Rama Hare Rama, Rama Rama, Hare Hare*. One day, the doctor went to a friend who had a female parrot that used to swear a lot, and he was appalled. He said, "This parrot is using such harsh words, and I have two parrots that are so spiritual."

His friend suggested that if he left his female parrot with the doctor's parrots for a week or two, she might learn something – she might become more spiritual. The doctor thought that was not a bad idea at all. That, they would benefit much from it, too. So he took the swearing female parrot back home, and he left her in the cage with his parrots. The two parrots were going, *Hare Krishna Hare Krishna,* and then they saw the female parrot. One of them stopped, but the other one kept chanting, *Hare Krishna Hare Krishna, Krishna Krishna Hare Hare.* The one that stopped said, "Hey, man, shut up! Our prayers have been answered, we can calm down now."

We don't want to be like those spiritual parrots. Be absolutely clear: chanting is not done to have your prayers answered. You pray when you want something, you don't chant. You don't chant the Gayatri mantra or any kind of mantra to have your wishes granted. You chant a mantra because you want to invoke the divinity within; to gain immense inner strength; to constantly purify yourself. With that purification and inner strength, everything would become plain sailing. Maybe you wouldn't even need to pray.

A good prayer would never ask God for something, anyway. A good prayer would not say, "God, please give me this or that." This is begging, not praying. A good prayer would simply express gratitude. But let's say your "prayer" entails asking the divine in you or outside – or a deity of your belief – for safety or health or sound finances or whatever else you want. That's not praying, but if you are praying, then stick to praying. Don't shift to mantra chanting for this.

Mantra chanting is supposed to invigorate you and your consciousness, to stir things up. For a while after you take up mantra chanting, you are going to experience a kind of upheaval in your life – everything will become topsy-turvy in the beginning. Then you will start to align yourself. A mantra is not chanted to fulfill our desires – for that, you have other options.

Mulla Nasruddin met his friend after a long time. He offered to take Mulla out for a drink.

"No, I no longer drink," said Mulla.

"You don't drink anymore? Why? What's wrong?"

"I quit drinking."

"Fine," his friend said. "Let's at least have a smoke."

"Sorry, I quit smoking too."

"You quit?" his friend asked. "Is your health okay? Let's go to the casino then."

"I don't gamble anymore," Mulla said.

"But why?"

"Well, I had a girlfriend, and she told me that she would marry me only if I stopped fooling around and stopped drinking and smoking."

"Oh, when did you stop?"

"It's almost been a year."

"And are you married now?" his friend asked.

"No."

"Why not?"

"Well, after I became so good and sober," Mulla said, "I figured I had plenty of other options, and I did not have to marry her anymore."

Chanting is to sober up. And once you do that, a whole world of options will open up for you.

In my book on mantras, I have talked about various kinds of beads and how they are used for different sadhanas. Most rosaries will have 108 beads; the one at the top is the 109th bead. We don't chant on this bead. It is simply to mark the beginning or the ending, depending on which way you look at it. It's called the *sumeru*, and we don't actually cross the *sumeru* when we chant the mantra.

The first finger is called the *tamasic* finger, which means it represents the mode of darkness, ignorance – *tamoguna.* The second finger represents the mode of passion. The third finger, the ring finger, represents the mode of goodness. The first finger is kept away when we do any sattvic chanting, which is clean or chanting of the right-handed path. Chanting can be of *dakshinacara*, the right-handed path, or *vamachara*, the left-handed path. *Vamachara* is outside the scope of my current exposition.

We rest the rosary on the ring finger supported by the thumb, and the second finger is used to move the beads. The thumb is called Brahma.

Now when I am at the last bead, I should not cross the sumeru. Instead, I have to turn the beads around and start again. This is how we chant with beads. You are welcome, even in your daily lives, to put these beads around your neck once you have finished chanting. Or you can put them back in your bag or put the bag around your neck, or you can leave the bag out – that's your personal choice. There are no hard and fast rules here.

The main rule with chanting, though, is to not cross the *sumeru*. If you are chanting and you lose your focus and drop the beads within the bag, for example, don't try to find where you were. Just start from the beginning.

I don't usually advise my more advanced disciples to chant on beads, because when you chant on beads, there is a tendency to rush through the chants.

You might say, "Hey Swami, I did my round in three minutes!" This is quite pathetic; it's not an achievement at all. So usually, instead of chanting with beads – or even while chanting with beads – I set a minimum time (rather than a minimum count). Hence, my own six-or-seven-or-ten-hour stretches. If I say, "I am going to sit like this and chant for ten hours," my mind will not rush – my mind will say, "Oh, he has committed to ten hours' chanting," Even if I finish quickly, my mind will not disturb me sooner.

It's just a matter of awareness. Because believe me, if you don't chant with awareness, you'll say, "Thank God, one more round done. Now, let me move to the next one." It should not be like this. It is not going to be enjoyable in the beginning but it should not be a torture either, so you should kind of like it.

Anyway, beads can be powerful reminders. In some sense, they're a little like robes. My guru, Naga Baba, used to say that wearing a robe is like a speed breaker: You won't go to a cinema, a theatre or a restaurant while wearing a robe – although we go to restaurants all the time, and don't feel out of place. But at least, as he said, there are many places you would automatically avoid while wearing a robe.

All religions of the world have certain symbols, and those symbols are there to remind us, whether it's a hat of some kind, a turban, something we wear around our necks, beads, a cross or a Star of David, or whatever. They are there to remind us of how we ought to lead our lives; what kind of principles we have committed ourselves to. Such as it is with the beads when you wear them – they remind you what you stand for.

To summarize, you can use beads in the beginning, and once you are finished chanting, you can wear them. Some people will write down this question tomorrow and ask me if I don't answer it today: If you go to the washroom, can you wear your beads? And in certain kinds of acts can you wear the beads? And so on. By all means, it's up to you. I don't want to saddle you with more rules. I am here to simplify everything on the path of mantra sadhana.

Very few people fall in love with their chanting, with their beads. For those lucky few who do, taking out your rosary and chanting your beautiful mantra is one of the most peaceful activities you can undertake.

Three Forms of Mantra Sadhana

All mantra sadhana falls into three categories. The first is called *nitya karma*. *Nitya* means something that's done routinely. *Nitya karma* is like attending school: you put on a uniform, go there and mark your presence. Though in itself this has some relevance, it doesn't mean much per se. But you go to school, get familiar with the learning environment, see other children, and so on.

Nitya karma is what a seeker does on a regular basis: it is refreshing your mind, practicing what you already know, every day.

Ramakrishna Paramahansa had three gurus; one of his gurus was a Naga saint named Totapuri.

Ramakrishna once asked him, "You have attained *nirvikalpa samadhi*, that rare and arguably the highest form or emancipation. why, then, do you still meditate?"

"You see that water pot?" Totapuri pointed to his water pot, which was made of brass, and said, "If you don't wash it daily, it gathers stains and spots. Therefore, I meditate a little every day to sustain the purification that I have done with intense sadhana."

You should make what you do sitting in front of an altar part of your routine; make it your daily discipline so that you refresh what you already know. That, however, does not usually give you the power you may need from mantras for certain accomplishments.

For that, there is a different kind of sadhana called *naimaittika karma*. And it is what really differentiates an ascetic, an adept from an average seeker.

Naimittika karma is something that is done with a specific purpose in mind. Doing *naimittika karma* entails devoting a certain time for your sadhana. For example, you could say, "I am going to chant this mantra over the next 40 days, 1,25,000 times," or "I am going to chant it 2,00,000 times or 40,000 times," and so on and so forth. It is like a fixed deposit in your spiritual bank account. What you do during that period of time is what you accumulate for future use.

When you do *naimittika karma*, you will gain some energy from your chanting. One of the common mistakes that people make with mantra sadhana is that they become eager to use it. I will give you an example; I wasn't thinking of citing it earlier, but it is surely relevant.

In 1999, I initiated a very nice person, a householder, into a specific mantra. Let's call him Tarun.

"Somewhere," I said to him, "I'm taking a risk by initiating you in this mantra. The only thing I ask of you is that please don't use it without consulting me. There is a reason I am telling you this, because one day you will need it for something in your family, for one of your children."

"Is everything going to be all right?" Tarun asked.

"Yes, but we'll need the energy of this mantra."

About eight years later, one of his cousin's uncles, an old man, fell gravely ill. Tarun went to see him at the hospital and couldn't bear to see him suffering. He asked me if he could use the mantra to help the old man, so he could leave this world peacefully.

"This soul's departure is only a matter of time," I replied. "Save this power, you will need it." But he couldn't contain himself. In his next visit, he saw his cousin crying, and the uncle in great pain and he sat there and applied the mantra. This was in the morning.

At around 3 pm, the same day, his uncle left his body.

"I am sorry," Tarun said to me over the phone, "but I could not resist using the mantra. Since I did not use it for my own benefit – after all, I helped somebody – so I think it should be all right."

"While it is not untrue that you used the energy of the mantra for somebody else, it's not entirely true either, because you used it out of a sense of attachment," I contended. "There were other patients in the hospital. You did not go to other patients and say, 'I am liberating you.' You helped somebody to whom you were attached, one way or the other. So while that is commendable, that is not entirely selfless. Your emotions got the better of you, and you used your energy just like that."

Fast forward a few years, and a young person in his

family was diagnosed with cancer. Fortunately, with the right medical and spiritual intervention, this storm passed.

With great power comes great responsibility. Uncle Ben in *Spiderman* said that – one wise fellow.

If you are going to accumulate energy, you also have a great responsibility to not use it just for yourself. It would be ideal also to confine yourself to using it for those to whom you are not connected, or at least use it for some people whom you do not know. This requires great mindfulness, because when you look around, everybody is disturbed or in pain in one way or the other. Everyone is in need. How you intervene makes a great deal of difference to yours as well as that person's life, because if you are interfering in the play of nature, somewhere, you must pay the price. Your intervention has to be done in accordance with nature, which is part of *naimaittika karma*.

Under *naimaittika karma* is a concept called *purushcharana*. *Purushcharana* is invoking a mantra and saving its energy for future use. It is always done over a specific period of time, and later in this book, I share the steps of *purushcharana*. Once you have done the *purushcharana*, you have accumulated the necessary spiritual wealth. Then, the third step is *kamya prayoga*.

Kamya means desired or desirable and *prayoga* means application. When you use that mantra for a certain application, that is *kamya prayoga*. Of these three aspects of mantra science, the second, *naimaittika karma*, is the most important and the primary focus of this book.

Performing the Gayatri Sadhana

One amazing thing about performing the Gayatri sadhana is that you notice a general rise in your body temperature within the first few days of starting your *purushcharana*. Don't be alarmed if that happens. Chanting the Gayatri mantra stimulates the solar channel in our body. Savitur Gayatri, the mantra we are concerned with in this book, has since times immemorial been chanted while standing in the river. For, *savitur* also means sun. Offering libations towards the sun while standing in water is an age-old practice.

Gayatri worshippers would chant this mantra while standing in a river, lake or an ocean, with water sometimes up to their knees, waists, or even up to their chests, depending on which lineage they belonged to. This is not just physical but psychical heat. The Tibetans call it *tummo*. I have found that what they do with a set of yogic practices to stimulate *tummo*, Gayatri mantra accomplishes a nearly similar outcome plus more.

From first-hand experience, I can confirm this mantra

generates heat in your body. Once when I was in Canada, I had some time to myself – this was before I renounced. It was a Wednesday afternoon, and I had a meeting on a Friday; I heard from my client that the meeting would be postponed to the following Tuesday. I thought, I now had Thursday, Friday, Saturday, Sunday and Monday free, and I didn't want to sit at home and do nothing or just play golf, etc.

Intending to make good use of my time, I decided to go away and do a little *purushcharana* of the Gayatri mantra. It obviously wasn't my first sadhana – I had done many *purushcharanas* by then and I knew how long I could sit, etc. So I figured I would chant the mantra up to 12 hours a day: three stretches of four hours, interspersed with three-hour breaks. I looked online for suitable places to avoid chanting at home or in a hotel room – I wanted a quiet, secluded place.

Fortunately, I found a rental caravan advertised on some website, so I left a message right away but no one called back. After waiting another couple of hours, I found two more places and left messages on their voicemails. No one called back. Meanwhile, it was evening and I went to play badminton. I thought why to waste my evening waiting for a phone call. It was better to get some blood circulation going.

Three hours later, when I finished and turned my phone on, there was a message on it from the caravan lady. It was nearly 8 pm by then. I called her back and she said, "Okay, you can take that place, no problem. But nobody lives there; it's totally isolated. Are you aware of that?"

"Yes," I said.

"And there's no running water."

"No problem."

"No flushing toilet either."

"Uh... okay... no problem."

"It's next to a lake, far into the woods."

"Sounds pretty nice!"

"Come to my place first," she said, "give me the money, then I'll give you the key."

It was only 50 bucks a day.

"Fair enough," I said to her.

I went home and said to my brother – and sister in-law, who always took care of me as a mother would – "I am going away for a few days." They were quite used to me heading off on the spur of the moment. My sister-in-law quickly said, "Let me at least pack a quilt for you and something to eat."

I said, "I won't be eating anything; don't bother packing any stuff for me."

I drove for hours. This place was quite far, and I put it on my GPS. It was way off the beaten track, and the GPS was going haywire. I was feeling bad for driving my brother's BMW on these unpaved roads. Somehow, I managed to reach the owner's place after midnight. I knocked on her door, and she said, "I am quite intrigued, because just last week I lost my sister, and she used to spend a fair bit of time in that caravan. Then I got a message from you saying you would like to rent my caravan for meditation. This must be God's mysterious way and not a coincidence."

The caravan was 20 minutes away from her place, she

told me, and that it was not locked and that there was no key because no one went there. But now that I was at her place, I could give her the rent first.

"Tomorrow morning you can drive back here," she said. "I can give you bread, milk and juice or something."

"Don't worry," I said. "I won't be eating anything. I have a bottle of orange juice." I had decided that I would take three sips of orange juice a day.

"Are you sure?"

"Positive."

"Well, if you change your mind, just give me a call. Don't die, you know."

I chuckled and said, "I'll be fine!"

I went to the caravan and lay down. I thought I would chant for an hour but I was very tired from first playing badminton and then driving for four hours, so I slept after a mere 20 minutes and woke up three hours later, at 4 am. I went to the lake – just remember, I don't know how to swim, so getting to the lake and filling a bucket for my bath while making sure I didn't slip into the water was not easy. Nevertheless, I managed. I bathed outside and took another bucket of water back to the caravan, and started my chanting.

The day went well. At night, during my rest period, I felt somebody wearing a hood was looking right at me through the little window of the caravan.

"Who's there?" I said. Nobody answered.

"Who's there?" I said again. Still nobody answered.

I flashed a light through the window, but in the pitch darkness outside the flash just glared back at me from the window pane. I heard some noise outside as if somebody was running. I got up quickly and opened the door of the caravan, and in the meantime, whatever this figure was just ran away; I couldn't catch a glimpse of anything.

Now that I am up, I thought, I might as well do some more chanting. So I chanted the whole night, and did so also for the third night. When I ended my sadhana on Monday morning, something beautiful happened. Before I tell you what happened, let me say that I don't want you to believe that something supernatural occurred, although I have experienced many such things in my life. This was simply beautiful. I had to do a little *yagna*. Now for the *yagna*, I did not have the firewood, nor did I have the permission to light a fire there. was Also, I wasn't carrying any ingredients for the *yagna*. I just wanted to light a little fire.

Luckily, I had taken some matchboxes with me. I broke off the heads, and the matchsticks became my tiny pieces of firewood. So I did a little *yagna* outside and when I finished and looked up, there was the most glorious sight of 40 or 50 lotuses by the bank of the lake nearby. They were in full bloom, with pink blossoms and sea-green pads, bathed in gentle sunlight – it was just delightful. I felt that my sadhana was complete. I have no clue why I failed to notice them on the first two days.

I should not use the word sadhana – it was more a mini *anushthana* but because it was the Gayatri mantra, the heat in my body was so great that I did not know what to do. I lost all my appetite because when there is excessive heat in the body, you tend to lose your appetite. I drove back home, and I didn't feel hungry that day or the next day. I just wanted to lie down but my mind was active, and my body energetic. I really couldn't do much.

The Gayatri mantra is one of the reasons I could live in the Himalayas wearing robes as the kind I wear – all cotton. This is actually more clothing than I wore in Badrinath during my sadhana. I was just in my loincloth, and the cold there did not bother me in the slightest. This is because the Gayatri mantra fires up the solar channel in your body.

If you feel excessive heat in your body when you chant the Gayatri mantra, it is important to lie down on your right side for a little while because when you lie down on your right side, your left channel, which is your lunar channel, will be activated. You will start to breathe from your left nostril and when you breathe from your left, you will cool down somewhat.

Next time you are angry or agitated, check if you are breathing from the left or right. In meditation, when you experience restlessness or aggressive thoughts, make sure you are breathing from the left – you will feel a calming sensation within a few minutes. If you are feeling lazy, breathe from the right nostril and this will invigorate you.

Invoking the Gayatri mantra in a structured manner will help you build a reservoir of divine energy. Let me go over that.

Specifics of Gayatri Sadhana

How Long Does It Take?

There are many ways to accumulate the energy of the Gayatri mantra in your consciousness. How long it takes for you to complete the sadhana depends on what kind of *purushcharana* you undertake. At the end of the day, the idea is quite simple: the more you gather, the more you have available for use at a later date. However, not everyone has the time or the inclination to undertake a long *purushcharana*. Irrespective of how little or much you do, the important thing to bear in mind is that the quantity of *japa* should be the same every day throughout your *purushcharana*.

Laghu Purushcharana (Mini Invocation)

3–9 days

Mini invocation is done over a minimum period of three days to a maximum of nine. Many people do it for nine days during the Navaratras, for example. When undertaking *laghu purushcharana*, you are required to do a minimum chanting of 1000 every day. The more the better as long as you maintain the same quantity every day. Doing it during the Navaratras is particularly auspicious and you can consult *panchangam* online or ask any Vedic scholar about the dates of the Navaratras that change every year.

Sadharana Purushcharana (Standard Invocation)

40–120 days

This is the ordinary kind of *purushcharana*. That's not to say that it doesn't have an impact – it does. More than first one and less than the next one. It is called ordinary or standard *purushcharana* because this is the bare minimum you need to do before you can start accumulating the energy of the Gayatri mantra. In the standard invocation, you chant the mantra a minimum of 100,000 times. Ideally, this should be done over a period of 40 days, which means you could chant approximately 2500 times every day for 40 days. If you are not doing *yajna* or the other post-*japa* rituals, then it is recommended to chant 3000 times every day for 40 days. It is also permissible to do this over 60, 90 or 120 days depending on how much time you are able to devote on a daily basis.

I would like to remind you that the vow to do a *purushcharana* is taken before you begin one. Therefore, you maintain the same quantity every day. If you decide to do a 60-day *purushcharana* and chant 2000 times on the first day, that consistency then must be maintained for the remaining 59 days. You can't change your 60-day *purushcharana* to a 120-day or a 40-day one once you've begun it.

Asadharana Purushcharana (Extraordinary Invocation)

18–24 months

Very few people undertake this kind of *purushcharana*. In fact, over the last three decades, I've met only three people who have done this kind. It involves chanting the Gayatri mantra 2,400,000 (24 lacs) times over a period of 18 or 24 months.

The *japa* is pegged at 24 lacs because the Gayatri mantra has what we call 24 *varnas*. Those are: *tat, sa, vi, tur, va, re, na, yam, bhar, go, de, va, sya, dhi, ma, hi, dhi, yo, yo, na, pra, cho, da* and *yat*. Mantra science dictates that to really invoke the energy of a mantra, you have to chant as many lacs of times as there are *varnas* in a mantra – not letters, but *varnas*, which roughly equate to syllables.

Maha Purushcharana (Grand Invocation)

24–32 months

This is the ultimate form of *purushcharana* and I've only known one person who did this 19 times in his life. Shriram Sharma of Shanti Kunj, Haridwar, was said to have done Gayatri Maha Purushcharana multiple times. The story of the person I wrote in the chapter 'The Power of Gayatri Mantra' was a direct disciple of Shriram Sharma.

In Maha Purushcharana, the Gayatri mantra is chanted 32 lacs or 3,200,000 times because when we add *Om-bhur-*

bhuva-svaha to the original Gayatri mantra found in the *Rig Veda* (3.62.10), the complete mantra has 24 *varnas*. They are 24 as explained earlier plus *a*, *u*, *m* (for *Om*), *bhu*, *bhu*, *va*, *sva* and *ha*.

The maximum period allowed to do a Maha Purushcharana is 32 months. There is no relaxation of rules for the longer *purushcharana*. The same principles of diet, abstinence and conduct apply to all four types. I must remind you here that just reckless or mindless chanting has no place or respect in mantra yoga. Your chanting must be done with devotion and mindfulness. I cannot stress this point enough. When you sit down to chant, do so patiently and mindfully, listening to your own voice, every word, every letter of your mantra. It will get tiring at times, but keep going if you care to go till the end.

The one who does 32 lakhs of *japa* of the Gayatri mantra is bound to have the grace of Devi in immeasurable, inexplicable ways. New dimensions of consciousness, new ways of thinking and new areas of knowledge and wisdom opens up to anyone who does this *purushcharana*, and if you do so with devotion, you will also attain what we call *vak siddhi*. *Vak siddhi* means when you say something from your heart, it becomes the truth; indeed, everything you say from your heart becomes the truth. That's how our sages achieved an exalted state in their own lifetimes.

When Can You Start This Sadhana

You can start Gayatri sadhana on any full moon day. You can carry out the routine in the morning or at night.

Praying to the Divine Mother in the form of Gayatri in the morning is the Vedic worship while the exact same routine, when undertaken at night, becomes Her tantric method of worship. The main thing is to be consistent. If you start a *purushcharana* by doing just one session of chanting in the morning, follow that till you complete the *purushcharana*. If you start your sadhana by chanting only in the evening, stick to that till the end. It is also perfectly fine to split your session into morning and evenings. Once again, if you do that, make sure you follow the same routine till you finish your *purushcharana*. Please note that at the beginning of every session, you've to do purification, *nyasa* and all the other steps as specified later in this chapter. Of course, you only have to perform the seven steps if you choose the brief invocation over comprehensive invocation. The idea is to train your mind by doing the same thing at precisely the same time for the same amount of minutes or hours every day for a certain length of duration.

Who Can Do This Sadhana

Any person, of any age, religion, ability or background can do this sadhana with or without initiation. Menstruating women can start or continue their sadhana without any reservations whatsoever. Complete abstinence must be practiced throughout the *purushcharana*. There's no *dosha* (issue) in case of wet dreams or any other involuntary release of sexual fluids. Voluntarily though, any form of sexual gratification is forbidden.

Diet

Throughout your *purushcharana,* you should be on a strict vegetarian diet. Dairy is allowed but no meat, seafood or eggs. No onion or garlic either. Be careful of eating biscuits, cakes, cheeses and supplements that may contain animal-derived ingredients. If your doctor has prescribed any medication, feel free to take it without any of the considerations above.

Lamp

Ideally, the lamp used in this *purushcharana* should be made of brass. An earthen lamp or a silver lamp can also be used. The wick must be of cotton. It is permissible to use braided cotton thread (like the common sacred red thread, *mauli*, for example, or any other) to use as a wick. The oil used in the lamp should be either ghee or sesame oil. If you are doing this sadhana in winters in a cold region, I would recommend using sesame oil as ghee solidifies very quickly and it may put out your lamp. Once again, it's important to be consistent. If you start your sadhana by lighting a ghee lamp, stick to that throughout your *purushcharana.*

Direction

The aspirant should face east, north or northeast while doing the chanting and the *yajna.*

Clothing

Any color is okay but the best are red, yellow and white. Ideally, you should wear no more than two pieces of red, yellow or white, loose-cloth on your body — one to cover your lower body and the other to cover the upper part. If you are in a very cold place, you can either use a heater in your room or sew your upper cloth with a woolen shawl. Women can wear a saree, blouse, etc.

Beads Bag (*Gomukha*)

If you use chanting beads, then I recommend using a bead bag called *gomukha*. Most of you would know how to use the *gomukha*. It's got two openings; one is larger than the other. It is designed so when you put the rosary in it, the beads don't touch the ground or dirty hands, and are kept pure.

You can wear it around your head if you like. Then you chant with the beads inside it, the index finger, however, remains outside the smaller opening of the *gomukha*.

Seat

The best seat will be a blanket on which you should spread the same colored cloth you cover your body with. Or, if you are wearing regular clothes (and not one of the three colors mentioned in the previous section) while doing *purushcharana*, you can just put a yellow cloth on your seat. The nature of this sadhana requires you to sit on the floor. If you are unable to do that, you may try sitting in a chair and setting up a table in front of you with lamp, pots, etc.

Personally, I have never experimented with that. If you do, please feel free to share the results of your sadhana.

Other than a blanket, you can also take a standard meditation cushion or use any seat made from cotton.

A seat made out of *kusha* grass is also permissible for this sadhana.

Posture

Try to maintain stillness of your posture while you chant with utmost mindfulness, faith and devotion. Please allow me to remind you that mantra sadhana is not about reckless chanting of a mantra just for the sake of ticking off an item in your list. It is the soulful process of becoming one with your deity so you may elevate yourself spiritually, materially and emotionally.

Things You Will Need to for Gayatri Sadhana

1. A lamp (brass, silver, or earthen)
2. Ghee or sesame oil and wick for your lamp
3. Five small water pots, a small spoon and a saucer if you are performing the comprehensive invocation or only one water pot if it's a brief invocation. The pots can be of silver, copper or brass. This is the standard for every sadhana and details on how to layout the pots (*patra*) can be found in the chapter 'Arrangement of Pots (*Patrasadan*)' in 'Detailed Notes'.
4. Standard ingredients for fire offerings (*yajna*) as mentioned in the chapter 'How to Make Fire Offerings (*Yajna*)'.

5. In addition to those ingredients, you will need firewood. You can use either wood from a sacred fig (Ficus *religiosa*. Common name: *Peepul*), mango (Magnifera *indica*, Common name: *Aam* or *aamra*) or *palasha* (Butea *monosperma*. Common name: *Plasha* or *dhak*). You can also use the wood from *deodar* (Cedrus *deodara*. Common name: *Devadaru*) or teak (Tectona *grandis*. Common name: *Sagaun* or *sheesham*).
6. Chanting beads made from rudraksha
7. A lot of faith, devotion and discipline

I strongly recommend that after going through this chapter, you make a daily checklist in line with the 36 steps I enumerate below. Also, make a daily list of what all you require; it's better to procure everything in advance.

The Mantra

Sanskrit (Devanagari)	*Sanskrit (IAST)*
ॐ भूर्भुवः स्वः तत्सवितुर्वरेण्यम भर्गो देवस्य धीमहि। धियो यो नः प्रचोदयात॥	oṃ bhūrbhuvaḥ svaḥ tatsaviturvareṇyama bhargo devasya dhīmahi । dhiyo yo naḥ pracodayāta ॥

Before You Begin

We must seek permission from the Divine Mother before undertaking Her sadhana. The simplest way to do this is to take a bath and sit at your altar after sunset. Take a bit of water in your right hand and mentally call upon the Divine Mother in the form of Gayatri and seek permission that may She and other forces of nature allow you to complete Her sadhana. Leave the water in the plate next to you.

Next, do 3, 7, 10 or 30 rounds of the Gayatri mantra chanting for mini, standard, extraordinary and grand invocation respectively. Use rudraksha beads. Use the same beads to commence your *purushcharana* the next day.

One round is 108 times. Thirty rounds will be chanting your mantra 108 × 30 = 3240 times, for example. Personally, I always chant 10,000 times before doing any major *purushcharana*. Once done, go to sleep in the same place where you chanted the Gayatri mantra. Here's the mantra again for your reference.

Sanskrit (Devanagari)	*Sanskrit (IAST)*
ॐ भूर्भुवः स्वः तत्सवितुर्वरेण्यम भर्गो देवस्य धीमहि। धियो यो नः प्रचोदयात॥	oṃ bhūrbhuvaḥ svaḥ tatsaviturvareṇyama bhargo devasya dhīmahi । dhiyo yo naḥ pracodayāta ॥
Translation	
May we abide in the Supreme Energy that is eternal, transcendental, radiant, perfect, divine. May such divine grace always guide us on the path of righteousness.	

How to Perform the Rites of Invocation (*Purushcharana*)

In this book, I have shared two methods of invocation: Comprehensive and Brief. Comprehensive is for seekers who are able to devote more time to sadhana. I recommend comprehensive method but someone invoking with the right sentiment will benefit just as much from the brief invocation as well. By right sentiment I mean that while chanting they are mindful, devotional and hopeful.

Essentials Steps in Gayatri Sadhana

The comprehensive invocation has 36 steps while the brief method has only 7 steps.

To perform so many steps in chanting the mantra might seem a little daunting in the beginning, but don't worry, first, we'll cover all the steps, so you know how to do each step, and then we can see which ones we can do without. Some things in many of the steps below may sound like rituals. Well, that's because they are. As I said earlier, first let me tell you everything, and then you can always cut out what you don't like. Besides, in case you don't want to go the immersive way, you can adopt the shorter route of just seven steps described at the end of this chapter.

Please note that the mantras used in this chapter are for your reference only. Their correct Sanskrit transliteration (for better phonetic accuracy) is given in the appendix. The pictures for various mudras too are in the appendix. (The description and meanings given in the appendix have been quoted verbatim from my book *The Ancient Science of Mantras*). The purpose of this chapter is to help you get familiar with all the steps but when you decide to do the actual sadhana, it is the information in the appendix you'll use directly.

The Comprehensive Method

Step One

The first step is bathing. Remember your mother used to tell you when you were growing up, "Take a shower, take a shower"? And you would say, "No, I don't feel like it today," and you would not listen (just kidding). I am telling you the exact same thing. I read this book, *All I Really Need to Know I Learnt in Kindergarten.* This is so true. All the basic human values have already been taught to us by the time we are just five-or-six-years old. You know: share your stuff, say grace, don't tell lies, go to bed on time and wake up early, and so on.

The first thing is bathing in the morning and it begins by showing two mudras. Fill a bucket of water if you take bath using a bucket or simply display the two mudras below under the shower (if you bathe by stepping into the shower).

Kalasha Mudra

Kalasha means a vessel, a pot, a *ghat*. This has come from my lineage of siddhas. Form a fist with your left hand and hold it with your right hand (wrap your left hand with your right).

Some people begin their day, not with *kalasha mudra* but *kalesha mudra. Kalesha* is the Sanskrit word for mental afflictions. They start their day thinking what is not right in their life. Stay with *kalasha*.

Form a fist with your left hand and cover it with your right hand. This is the most simple *kalasha mudra*. On that, we form a *matsya mudra*, which is called the forming of a fish. This is with the left hand at the bottom and right hand on top. This is the fish – don't eat it. Now you have filled the bucket with water, performed the *kalasha mudra* and the *matsya mudra*.

Matsya Mudra

Matysa means fish. Stretch your left hand, palm facing downwards and thumb pointing out. Put your right hand on top, once again, palm facing downwards and thumb pointing out. Just twiddle your thumbs a bit and the *matsya mudra* is complete. (*Matsya mudra* is shown in the appendix).

One of Vishnu's first incarnation was a *matsya*. The idea is that by showing these two mudras, we get in touch with our primordial source.

Now chant the following mantra:

Ganga cha yamune caiva godavari Sarasvati,
Narmade sindhu kaveri jalesmina samnidhima kuru.

When we chant this with devotional sentiment, we are inviting the energy of all the holy rivers into our water – that while I am unable to bathe in the rivers stated in our scriptures, where our sages once bathed, I am invoking the energy of these rivers in the bath I am now going to take.

It is essential to invoke that sentiment inside you. A lot boils down to your sentiment and faith in mantras. Yesterday, a gentleman raised a beautiful question about faith: Is faith really necessary in mantras? Yes, it is. Because invoking the energy of a mantra is not about brute chanting of it, but connecting your consciousness with a higher source. Faith makes it easier. Faith is love. It is hope.

I once read a quote: "Across the gateway of my heart I wrote: 'No Thoroughfare', But love came laughing by, and cried, 'I enter everywhere.'" Faith is similar. It doesn't matter how much you resist, once you purify yourself and lead a life of purpose, faith just makes its way into your heart. It's like your favourite pet dog who wants to sit next to you – it just barges in and leans against you.

Step Two

The second step is to put on fresh clothes. Some people keep a separate set of clothes for their daily puja, and they don't wear them anywhere else which is quite good but I have also seen some lazy ones, who would wear their clothes for a puja and hang them on a hook and then the next day take them off and wear them again. They will say, "These are my puja clothes," but they might not wash them for 30, 40 or 50 days. Believe me, I know such people. Don't do that. Put on fresh clothes.

There is a story I wrote on my blog some time ago. Once Buddha was in solitude, walking, he asked for alms from a man. The man refused and started shouting at him, calling him names. Buddha did not say anything, and went on his way quietly.

Another man who was observing this went to the man and said, "You just insulted the Buddha."

The man said, "That beggar couldn't possibly be Buddha."

The observer said, "No, he was!"

"But Buddha is always surrounded by people."

"Well, he's in his stint of solitude."

Repenting his actions, he went looking for Buddha, but couldn't trace him. The next day, however, he found him, and fell at his feet.

"O Lord!" he said remorsefully. "I am sorry I insulted you and called you names."

"Oh, when was that?" Buddha said calmly.

"Just yesterday!"

'Tathagata does not know yesterday," Buddha said. "I only know today, this moment."

Besides hygiene, the idea of bathing and putting on fresh clothes is so you allow yourself to have a fresh start for the day. It is a golden opportunity, a divine blessing that you have one more day to live, one more moment to breathe. I read somewhere that if we were to live every day as if it is our last day, one day, we are most certainly going to be right. So put on fresh clothes.

Step Three

Now you enter the puja *griha*, the sanctum sanctorum, or stand before the altar. If you have a separate puja room or just a little space, how do you approach it? You are entering your sacred space. Like your washroom is where you perform physical cleansing, your altar is for your spiritual cleansing. There is a mantra that you can chant. It's *Om Hrim Astraya Phat*. When you say *phat*, you are supposed to stamp the floor with your heel. In earlier times, they used to do this because floors were sealed with cow dung and the like. Thus, there would be some microorganisms on the floor of your sanctum sanctorum, and by stamping your heel on the floor, you would shake the surface so they could move; so you don't step on them.

How do you pronounce these seed syllables? Is it 'hring', or is it 'hrim'? For that, I would give you a simple rule of thumb – the elaborate method is a little complicated, and this is not the forum for that. But quite simply, how do you say the word 'maa' (the Hindi or Sanskrit word for mother)? When you say the word 'maa', there is a nasal sound at the end. You don't say 'maam', you don't say 'maang' – you say 'maa'. Similarly, the word is 'hrim' ('m' being the same soft nasal sound as in the word 'maa') and not 'hring'.

If I have to pronounce an 'm' sound at the end, I will not write an 'm'. I will simply have what we call an *anuswar*, a dot. The *anuswar* denotes a purely nasal sound, so you would say 'hrim' – there is no 'g' – but a nasal sound where there is a lurking 'g' sound, as in *Om Hrim Astraya Phat*. I can't think of another way to explain this in written English.

Step Four

Step four is performing the purification ritual. You would have a little vessel of water – you just dip your finger in it.

Remember, the index finger represents ignorance. In the invocation of mantras, as in all spiritual, religious karma, we keep this finger away. To perform purification, either take a flower in your hand, holding it with your thumb and three fingers (except the index finger) or simply join the ring finger with the thumb if you are not using a flower. Now take a little pot of water. You dip ring finger joined with your thumb, or if you have a flower, you can dip your flower, in the water and chant the mantra:

Om apavitrah pavitro va
sarvavastham gato api va
yah smaret pundarikaksam
Sa bahaya abhyantaram sucih

As you are doing that, sprinkle some water in all the ten directions. You don't count, one, two, three, four, five, six, etc. – just do so symbolically.

This mantra expresses that even though I have taken a bath and put on fresh clothes, there are still impurities I carry on my body, in my heart and my mind, which are to be removed by meditating on the divine energy. The meaning of this mantra is given below:

Om apavitrah pavitro va
Sarvavastham gato api va

It does not matter how impure you are; in whatever state you may be.

Yah smaret pundarikaksam
sa bahaya abhyantaram sucih

The one who meditates on the divine energy – the Lord is called *pundarikaksha* here, with beautiful lotus eyes – the one who meditates on such form of the Lord is purified inside out.

This mantra does not give you an excuse to not bathe, but it will purify you, so do it with that sentiment.

Step Five

Having purified the surroundings, we now do the next level of purification by doing *achamana. Achamana* is to drink three small sips of water from your water pot. It is done three times to signify purification of your body, mind and consciousness. When we chant the Gayatri mantra, we say *bhurbhuvah svah. Bhur* means this plane of existence; *bhuvah*, the plane of consciousness, and *svah* the plane of the soul. The three states of consciousness are the dreaming, waking and sleeping states. This is why we say *bhur bhuvah svah* three times.

Although many ancient and medieval texts go into great detail on how *achamana* should be performed, and how people belonging to different castes are supposed to do it, in the science of mantras, those rules don't apply. Because the moment you are initiated, you don't belong to a particular caste, or anything: You belong to that lineage.

Here I'll digress for a moment to tell you about the role of initiation, or why initiation is considered almost sacred on the path of mantra yoga. At the same time, I don't want to overstate the importance of initiation either: I don't want to give you the idea that getting initiated is the end of your sadhana or that without it you can't succeed. This is not the case.

Having said that, initiation does bestow a certain power on your chanting. Imagine you run a government department – let's say you are a minister and you hold a certain portfolio. Somebody comes to you seeking help saying, "I have to speak to a manager in your department." You might tell him, "No problem, here is my recommendation letter – take it, and give it to the relevant manager." The manager will see your signature and say, "I know the minister has sent him, and okay, I'll do what he asks." Being initiated is something like this.

When you connect to a lineage, all the *siddhas*, the adepts before you have made certain recommendations, and there is a collective karma that you get to tap into. While Steve Jobs invented iPod and iPad, not everybody in Apple has to do the same. He generated a mountain of cash, and now they have access to that, because of his efforts, strategy and vision – his execution. Likewise, you get to benefit from what the seers before you do have said and done in your lineage.

There is a story I once read in a book written by Pandit Rajmani Tigunait,* a disciple of Swami Rama. He wanted

---

* It was more than 10 years ago when I read that book. I can't seem to find it on my bookshelf. I am 99.9% certain that the book I read it in was *Power of Mantra and the Mystery of Initiation* by Pandit Rajmani Tigunait.

to chant a particular verse from a text called *Soundarya Lahari*, which is from the Sri Vidya tradition. In that text, for every verse you can do a *purushcharana;* you can invoke and accumulate energy.

Pandit Rajmani chanted a particular mantra without telling his guru, and his chanting had no effect. One day, Swami Rama came back from a tour and asked him to bring him his copy of *Soundarya Lahari.* Of all the mantras, he pointed to that particular mantra, and said, "Chant this one." Pandit Rajmani thought, *I have already done this and it has had no effect.* He had tried chanting earlier, 11,000 times, 62,000 times and 1,25,000 times. Hiding his feelings and thoughts, he asked Swami Rama how much he should chant every day, to which Swami replied by saying that only ten times.

"Just one-zero, not ten thousand?" Pandit Rajmani exclaimed.

"Okay, if that doesn't seem enough," Swami Rama said, "you can chant it 1000 times a day."

Still in a state of disbelief, he asked, "Really? Just 1000 times"

"Well then, you can do 2000 times."

Pandit Rajmani realized that each time he questioned him, Swami Rama was simply increasing the number, so he stopped and did as he was told, and got the result that was promised in the text.

Forty days later, he went to Swami Rama, elated, and said, "Look, the results came through. I had the experience I was seeking. This is just remarkable!" But Swami Rama seemed upset with him. Pandit Rajmani couldn't understand why his guru would be unhappy, because he had just finished his sadhana.

Finally, Swami Rama clarified, "You see, before you joined our lineage, my guru, with the power of his *tapas*, his penance, had simplified this sadhana. It would only require somebody 10 chants each day. But now, anybody after you will need to do 2000 every day to achieve the same result. Due to your ego you questioned the number of rounds for chanting the mantra, and changed it unnecessarily."

When you connect with a lineage, it becomes your signature. If the *siddhas* have said, "This will happen when you chant this mantra," sooner or later, it will happen.

Presently, to perform *achamana*, you will need an *achamana* pot and vessel. They are very inexpensive but if you can't source them for any reason, just use any small pot and a little spoon. There's no hard and fast rule for this.

Take the spoon in your left hand, scoop up some water with it and pour that water in the palm of your right hand. Now say, "*Om Keshavaya Namah*" and then drink the water from your right palm. Do it once more saying "*Om Madhavaya Namah*" and repeat it while chanting "*Om Narayanaya Namah*".

So, three times all up. Once done, put some water again in your right palm, put the spoon in your left hand back in the pot, say, "*Om Pundarikakshaya Namah*", then wash your hands on the left side.

I hope you won't feel overwhelmed with all these mantras just because you don't know them. You see, nobody is born with knowledge. If you practice a few times, they will come to you. But if you say, "I don't want to chant any mantras at this point," that's okay too, it's not a deal breaker. You can still do your thing, without chanting a mantra here. For all I care, you could chant the Gayatri mantra itself for all these steps, if you really want to simplify it to the extreme. My personal recommendation, however, is that you go through these steps, make your own notes and follow them. Things will then flow effortlessly.

Step Six

Light a lamp now. You can light the lamp just as you would light a cigarette, that is, without any mantra and with the same eagerness. Or, you could take it a step further and chant a mantra and do it with devotion.

Om Agni Varchau Jyotir Varchau Svaha
Om Agni Jyotir Jyotir Agnih Swaha
Suryo Jyoti Jyotir Suryah Swaha
Agnir Varcho Jyotir Varchah Swaha
Suryo Varcho Jyotir Varchah Swaha
Jyoti Suryah Suryo Jyotih Swaha

Step Seven

Now, we invoke Ganesha. All Vedic, mantric, tantric and puranic pujas must begin with Ganapati. This is a scriptural injunction and there is a simple mantra, if you want to do a short one: *Om Ganeshaya namah.* That should do; that will make Ganesha happy – he is easily pleased. If you want to do a longer one, then you can do:

Vakratunda mahakaya suryakoti samaprabha
nirvighnam kurume dev sarvakaryesu sarvada ||

If you want an even longer one, which is the one I personally used during all of my sadhanas – I always did the longer Ganapati mantra along with the shorter ones – it would be:

Sumukhashch aikadantashcha kapilo gajkaranak
lambodarashch vikato vighnanaasho vinaayak
dhoomraketur ganaadhyaksho bhaalchandro gajaanan
Dvadashaitani namani yeh patheccharnuyadapi.
viddhya rambhe vivadhe cha praveshe nirgame tathaa
sangraame sankate chaive vighnastasya na jaayate.

There is more in the mantra, but it ends here for our purposes. It's really up to you whether to do the long or short mantra. You could simply say, *Om Ganeshaya Namah:* Thank you Ganesha, I can't say more than this, please be with me.

Once there were two people, and one of them was an ardent devotee. The whole day, he prayed to God. And the other was his neighbour, who prayed just twice a day: Just like "*Om Ganeshaya Namah*, thank you Ganesha, hope you are doing fine. I am well, thank you." In the morning and evening, that was his routine. When they died, the devotee who was chanting the glories of God all the time went to hell, and his neighbour went to heaven. The devotee said, "There has to be some mistake. I was the one who was chanting all the time, calling out to God. How did he get to heaven, and I end up in hell?"

God said, "He didn't bother me all the time."

So feel free to do a short mantra. The crucial thing is to have the correct sentiment in your heart when you chant it.

Step Eight

This is done by showing three mudras – handlocks – of Ganesha. I should briefly touch upon the role of mudras. If you are some distance away and I call out to you, you may or may not hear my voice. But if I wave my hand, you will see and say to yourself, "Oh, somebody is waving his hand – somebody is trying to call out to me." Mudras are something like that. They are called handlocks: gestures which are based on your lineage of *siddhas*; the adepts before you have championed them and the energies around you recognize that. If you want to view this more scientifically, then the flow of energies in the body is directed by way of mudras.

Step Nine

And then we do what we call, *swasti vachana*. *Swasti* means *kalyan*, auspiciousness, goodness, and *vachana* means talking or chanting. It would take you at least 10 to 15 minutes to chant a whole *swasti vachana*. But, I have taken the most important aspect of *swasti vachana* and shortened it for you. (The meaning and transliteration is given in the appendix).

> *Harihi Om Bhadram Karnebhih Shrnuyama devah |*
> *Bhadram pasyemaksabhiryajatrah*

Sthirairangaistustuvagamstanubhih
Vyasema devahitam yadayuh
Svasti na indro vrddhasravah
Svasti nah pusa visvavedah
Svasti nastaksaryo aristanemih
Svasti no bruhaspatirdadhatu|
Om Shantih Shantih Shantih

If you can't chant this, just read the translation. But even if you practice these mantras a little, you'll find the Vedic sound has a potent energy, because Sanskrit makes extensive use of two particular sounds: One is the 'm' sound, the other is the 'n' nasal sound. You can drag these sounds on for however long you wish. It's just 'hmm'. You can sing anything in Sanskrit.

You can sing all Sanskrit scriptures, barring perhaps a couple of Upanishads that written prosaically unlike all the rest that read poetically.

Step Ten

Now, it's time to meditate on your guru – to perform guru *dhyana*, or guru meditation. Usually, you meditate on your guru on your crown chakra, at the top of your head. My guru, Naga Baba, told me that when you meditate in the morning, you should imagine a very pleasing, smiling face of your guru. I had trouble doing that, because I rarely saw Baba smiling. In the images that I had in the photo album of my mind, Baba was mostly stern or angry, which one should I pick? Which one would do justice to him? I smiled a little to myself when Baba told me this, but I found some way of meditating on his smiling form.

The guru meditation is usually the first thing a good disciple does in the morning, even before he jumps out of bed and checks his phone messages. If you don't have a guru in human form, you can just visualize light or the deity of your mantra in the crown chakra. If you don't want to do that either because you have an affinity for a particular form or god, just visualize that god there – it doesn't matter which religion. The idea is to start your day with something good; to start your day with a soft, warm feeling in your heart.

Step Eleven

Now chant your guru mantra. The guru mantra is usually different from your sadhana mantra. Sometimes it can be the same if you are doing a sadhana of the guru mantra itself. If you don't have a guru and you don't have a guru mantra, you can simply chant the Gayatri mantra.

I urge you not to think that the absence of a guru mantra means you will not succeed. Gurus are important, but not indispensable. It's entirely in your hands. Please don't go looking for gurus – you will be disappointed. And please don't think, for example, that if you are fascinated with Devi worship and you get initiated in Sri Vidya, your progress will be assured. There are many people who would initiate you for 50 rupees. You may go to them for the first time, and say, "Initiate me," and they might say, "All right, take a seat."

Those initiations have nothing to offer. You are the maker of your destiny; you know the path, you know the science behind it. Just stick to your routine, do your practice and you will get there.

Step Twelve

In this step, we pay obeisance to all the *siddhas*. Your lineage may have different adepts that your guru may tell you to pay obeisance to, but if you don't belong to a lineage; if you haven't been initiated into Gayatri sadhana, you can simply say *Om Divyog Namah, Om Sidhyog Namah, Om Manavog Namah:* I offer my obeisance to all *siddhas* who are in divine, ethereal and human bodies.

The idea is to do each of these steps with humility in your heart.

Step Thirteen

Ishta generally means desired. *Ishta-devata* is the deity or the form of God you generally pray to. Your current sadhana may well be to invoke your *ishta* or it may be to attain mantra *siddhi* or some other divine entity. For example, on your usual days you may be praying to Krishna, etc., but now you are trying to invoke goddess Gayatri. In this case, your *ishta* is Krishna, whereas the deity of your mantra is Gayatri. Before you can awaken the mantra of your deity, an aspirant is required to meditate on his *ishta-devata* as well. If, however, the deity you are trying to invoke is your *ishta-devata*, simply meditate on the form of your *ishta*.

Your *ishta-devata* could be any god, goddess from any religion for that matter. Religion is not important in sadhana, for sadhana is a religion in its own right. If you pray to a specific god, pray to that diety now or simply meditate on Mother Goddess Gayatri using the mantra below.

> *Om balam vidyam tu gayatrim lohitam chaturananam,*
> *raktambaradvayopetamakshasutrakaram tatha.*
> *kamandaludharam devi hamsvahanasamsthitam,*
> *brahmani brahmadaivatyam brahmalokanivasinim.*
> *mantrenavahayeddevimayanti suryamandalat.*

Step Fourteen

Chant the mantra of the deity you visualized in the preceding step. Please note that this is not your main mantra. But, if your *ishta-devata* is the same as the deity of your mantra then, of course, you'll chant the same mantra. Ishta-mantra is to be chanted 11, 21 or 31 times.

Step Fifteen

Now we pray to Mother Earth by performing *prithvi* puja. It is important because we are sitting on the earth. In all forms of classical dance of India, we offer respects to earth before beginning with the main performance. I've known Ganesh, a Bharatanatyam dancer, for nearly five years now and when I watched him for the first time, I saw that before starting, he offered flowers to Mother Earth and sought forgiveness: that dear mother, I will be stomping on you and I might be causing you hurt by doing this, so please forgive me. It's such a beautiful sentiment – even dance becomes sadhana. This act of artistic expression becomes a spiritual activity because the sentiment behind it is, I want to pray and express my gratitude. Rather than chanting, somebody might offer his worship with dance; someone else might do it with painting, for example.

The usual way you perform *prithvi* puja is to take the water in a vessel, dip your ring finger in the water, and draw one line on the ground in front of you. You then draw another line, then another line to form an inward-pointing triangle. The same way, you take water once more and put a dot in the middle of this triangle.

The drawing on the ground, done with water will look as follows:

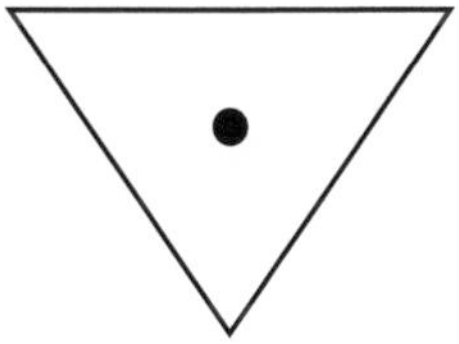

So you have taken water four times. That becomes a symbol of Devi, of Adhaar Shakti. *Adhaar* means foundation, the foundation energy. When we place the dot in the middle of the triangle, we chant the mantra *Hrim Adhaar Shakteya Namah. Hrim Adhaar Shaktaya Namah*, which means, I am offering my obeisance to Mother Earth, the foundation energy, and I am going to start my sadhana.

Take a moment to mentally express your gratitude to Mother Nature, Mother Earth, for blessing you with the privilege and that ground where you are able to sit now and invoke divine energies.

Step Sixteen

This is the one step that's performed only on the first day and is not repeated on any other day throughout your sadhana. Now, we take a *sankalpa*, a vow. When you take a *sankalpa*, you make a commitment with the universe that you are undertaking a certain practice with a particular intention. This is done only on the first day of the *purushcharana*.

When you take a vow and fulfill it, it boosts your willpower. To take a *sankalpa*, just pour a little water from your vessel into your right palm. If you have a flower, put the flower with it, a bit of rice if you have it – if you don't have rice, no problem. With your utmost sentiment, say to the Divine: "I, such-and-such person (if your guru has given you a name, this is the moment to use that name, because that will identify you with the lineage to which you belong), am taking a vow of chanting 'x' number of mantras over the next 'n' number of days. I'm doing this for the Grace of Vedmata Gayatri."

Or, if you have taken a *sankalpa* of chanting, let's say, one hour every day or 50 minutes every day, then you will say, "I, so-and-so, will chant Gayatri mantra for 'x' minutes/hours every day for the next 'n' number of days. I'm doing this for the Grace of Vedmata Gayatri."

Your *sankalpa* may be that, "I will chant the mantra of Vedmata Gayatri or the Gayatri mantra 'x' number of times, over the next 'y' number of days. And I am doing so because

I want 'z'." The best thing to say is, "I am doing so for Devi's grace," because in the beginning, you should accumulate the energy of the mantra. Don't say, "I am doing it because I want to win the lotto," or whatever. Accumulate the energy, because once you have enough, you can do *kamya prayoga* – you can actually use it for application.

When you violate your *sankalpa*, your sadhana is compromised and you must either start from the beginning or seek a remedial measure from your guru. For example, if in your *sankalpa*, you state that you will chant 4,000 mantras every day for the next 40 days but you miss one day or chant less one day, this compromises your sadhana. You must reset the counter and start all over again.

To do the *sankalpa*, simply take water in your right palm, put a few grains of rice and a flower and say it in any language you know. Fill in the blanks:

I ... *(your full name)* ... born in ... *(state your* gotra. *If you don't know your* gotra, *simply say* Narayana gotra *for everyone is a child of the Divine)* ... on ... *(state your date of birth)* hereby vow to do a *purushcharana* of ... *(the name of your mantra, like Gayatri, Sri Suktam, Guru Mantra, etc.)* ... over the next ... *(state the number of days you'll be chanting the mantra over, for example, 40, 90, 100, 300 and so on)* days ... so I may become a worthy recipient of your grace and attain the desired outcome.

After you have made your *sankalpa,* keep the water that you have in your palm, with your flower and rice, in a small plate in front of you and on that very day pour it on the base of any tree or plant. As I have written, avoid cactus – all other plants are fine.

Step Seventeen

Mantra *shvasa* is very simple: You breathe in while you are chanting your mantra, and you breathe out while chanting. On the first day, I recommend doing 21 times in the case of doing the small invocation, 1 round if you are doing the standard invocation, 3 rounds if you happen to perform the extraordinary invocation and 7 rounds in case you are doing the grand invocation. Remember that one round is 108 times. That's not chanting three times – it's three rounds.

On all subsequent days, do only 3, 11, 21 or 31 times for small, standard, extraordinary and grand invocations respectively.

While inhaling, you obviously cannot chant aloud. When you are inhaling, you can do one chant and while exhaling you can chant as well. This is called mantra *shvasa*. The counting mentioned in the earlier paragraph is not per *shvasa* but per chant. So 7 times means 4 exhalations and 3 inhalations. One exhalation is extra because you always start with exhalation.

It is possible to do an entire sadhana on just mantra *shvasa*. If you are used to mantra *shvasa*, or let's say, all you wish to do in your sadhana is mantra *shvasa*, then you take a vow like, "For the next 'x' days I am going to do mantra *shvasa*, 'y' rounds every day." You could be practicing it while walking, commuting or doing any other activity where you may do it with mindfulness. Mantra *shvasa* is a very effective practice, because you are chanting your mantra in your daily life. The more you chant with feeling, the more energy you accumulate. Bear in mind that it's like doing shift work: The more shifts you work, the more money you make. It will tire you out, but you will get used to mantra *shvasa* and you will continue to accumulate energy.

Step Eighteen

We'll now do *viniyoga*, means the application of the mantra. *Sankalpa* is done only once on the first day whereas *viniyoga* is done every day throughout your *purushcharana*. Here's the mantra for Gayatri *viniyoga*:

> *Saptavyahratinam jamadagni, bharadvaja, atri-gautama,*
> *kasyapa, visvamitra, vasistha rshayah,*
> *Gayatryusniganustubbrhati-pamk*
> *tistristubjagatyaschandadamsi,*
> *Agni-vayu-surya-brhspati-varunendra-visvedeva devatah,*
> *Sarvapapaksayarte Jape Viniyogah.*

Now don't be alarmed – you don't have to chant it. There is a simple way to do it: Take water in your palm and say, "O the sages who have existed before me who have invoked Vedmata Gayatri, I am chanting this to purge myself of all the bad karma I might have done, to cleanse myself of all the negative emotions I carry in my heart." After you have said this, just pour the water from your palm on the ground in front of you.

Step Nineteen

Now we come to the purification of the hands, which is called *kara shuddhi*. There's an old *bhajan* that says, "*Vadan diya hari gun gaane ko aur haath diye kar daan re...*" That we have been blessed with a mouth so we may sing His glories and hands so we may engage in charitable acts. But often in our lives we end up doing things with our hands that don't befit us. Before our hands perform *mudras* (handlocks) or *nyasa* (placement of letters of the mantra on our body), we need to purify our hands. The rationale is quite simple: can't wash off dirt with dirty water; we can't purify our body with impure hands.

Purification ritual is performed by chanting "*Om bhurbhuva svaha*" and washing your hands while you chant it. Three times the hands are washed and three times the same mantra is chanted.

Once again, you wash your hands by taking a bit of water in the right hand and then symbolically washing both hands with it to your left side. You can keep a small towel with you to wipe your hands every time you use water. This is completely at your discretion.

Now, chant the following mantras and show the appropriate mudras to perform purification of the hands.

Aing Anushthabhyam Namah.
Hring Tarjanabhyam Namah.
Shring Madhyamabhyam Namah.
Aing Anamkiabhyam Namah.
Hring Kanishkabhyam Namah.
Shring Kartakishtabhyam Namah.

We have placed little mantras on our hands. Now the feeling, the sentiment is that these are the hands of Devi – that Devi alone is fit to worship Herself.

Step Twenty

Two steps are of great importance when doing mantra sadhana. One is *nyasa* and the other *mudras*. *Nyasa* is the method by which you no longer remain a body, but become a mantra. The idea behind this is not simply purification of your body, mind and soul, but to become at par with the object of worship.

Let's say you invite a beggar into your home and tell him, "Please sit next to me at the dining table." This would likely make the beggar feel very uncomfortable. You might also feel awkward; you would feel more comfortable speaking to somebody on a similar wavelength. It would be easier to communicate; to spend time with that person.

So it is with chanting. With our petty thinking, our limited minds, we can't be at one with the object of our worship, our mantra, with our deity. This requires us to rise above the limited tendencies of the mind – our self-centredness, selfishness, jealousy, hatred, negativity and so on. This is invariably done while you are chanting the mantra, by *nyasa*, in which you place various letters of the mantra on your body. This way, the mantra is done with awareness, consciousness and devotion; through the *nyasa*, you become the mantra.

There are many kinds of *nyasas*. There is *rishyadi nyasa,* in which we pay homage to all the rishis, the sages of the lineage in our mantra who have invoked it in the past. Then we have the *varana nyasa* or *nyasa* on the syllables of the mantra, followed by *matrika nyasa,* which is in a Sanskrit script called Devanagari. (An ancient form of Sanskrit script was called Brahmi, which had more letters than Devanagari).

Since we did the purification of our hands in the previous step, we are now ready to invite the energy of the deity into your body. The mantras of the *nyasa* are covered in the appendix.

Then we do what is called the *pranava nyasa*. The sound '*Om*' is called *pranava*, from the original *prana*, the life force that has evolved. It is done as follows:

Om brahma rsaye namah sirasi|
Gayatrichanda se namah mukhe |
Om paramatmadevatayai namah hradi |
Viniyogaya namah sarvange |

Now that you have invoked the primordial vital life force in our body, you are ready to perform *nyasa* of the hands. Please note that this is not purification of the hands where we use seed syllables from the mantra.

Om tatsaviturbrahmane angusthabhyam namah |
Varenyam vishnave tarjanibhyam namah,
Om bhargo devasya rudraya madhyamabhyam namah |
Om dhimahi Isvaraya anamikabhyam namah |
Om dhiyo yo nah sadasivaya kanisthkabhyam namah |

It says *Om tatsavitur angushthe brahmane namah* – that these first words of the mantra have the energy of the Creator. The next words are *Varenyam, Vishnave. Varenyam* – means fit to be worshipped and fit to be adopted; has the energy of the one who is running the universe, namely, Vishnu. *Bhargo Devasya, Rudraye*: The energy of the deity Rudra in the words *Bhargo Devasya*, the destroyer, the destruction. We must destroy our negative thoughts; we hold onto our positive thoughts, our good emotions and always create good feelings, good thoughts and good things in the world.

Om dhimahi ishvaraye anamikabhyam namah: The energy of the all-pervading God, who is beyond forms. *Om dhiyo yo nah sadasivaya*: The one who bestows grace, *anugraha*. *Om pracodayata, sarvaatmane*: The one supreme soul which lives in all entities throughout all the universe, that carries the indivisible energy, the word *pracodayata*.

One of the reasons this mantra is so potent is because it carries all the energies in its various words.

Now we'll do what is called *Shadanga mantra nyasa*. As I said, please don't be overwhelmed by all this. Once you get used to it, it'll be a piece of cake. Besides, if you find this too much, you can always opt for the concise method.

Mantras for which you can do a sadhana usually have what is called *shadanga*, or six limbs. They are: The mantra itself, the *beej* or seed of that mantra. The energy of a mantra that doesn't have a seed cannot be used for a long time. *Devata*, the deity of that mantra; rishi, the original seer of that mantra; *chanda*, the meter of that mantra. Meter is usually the result of the arrangement of words and letters. In a mantra, it is this and how it's to be recited. And then you usually have *utkeelan*. Not all mantras have this. Some mantras have a specific seed syllable or word that you use as a password or passcode to unlock the power of that mantra. This is called *utkeelan*, because all mantras were *keelit*. *Keelit* means to nail something down. As I wrote in my book *The Ancient Science of Mantras*, when Shiva created all the mantras in the universe, they were locked, as it were, so that people could not misuse them for own their limited desires. And every mantra has what we call shakti, or energy. These are the *shadanga*, the six limbs or aspects of a mantra.

Om tatsaviturbrahmane Hradayaya Namah|
Om varenyam vishnave sirase svaha

Earlier, when you said *sirase*, you touched the top of your head. But in this, you just touch your forehead.

Om bhargo devasya rudraya sikhayai vasat |
Om dhimahi isvaraya kavacaya hum |
Om dhiyo yo nah sadasivaya netratrayaya vausat

Netratrayaya means three eyes – the two physical eyes, and the third, inner eye.

Om Pracodayat sarvatmane astraya phat|

Nyasa with exact mantras and mudras can be found in the appendix. If you wish to perform extended *nyasa* (like *varna nyasa,* etc.), that too I've provided there.

Step Twenty-One

This step is called *purva mantra japa* or preliminary mantra chanting and is done before you perform the mudras (the next step). You usually have to do the preliminary mantra chanting about 21 times. That will be more than sufficient. If you can't chant 21 times, do it 7 times – though I don't see why you can't chant 21 times.

While we are going through all this, you may think, why be so elaborate? Or, does this really have any meaning? Or, would mantras really benefit me in any way? I can tell you one thing: when you chant with devotion, it doesn't matter which mantra you chant – without a doubt, you are going to experience a different dimension of yourself.

Step Twenty-Two

The other means by which we can be at one with the object of our worship is mudras. As I was explaining yesterday, when you can't hear somebody, you can wave at him and he will still be able to see you. More than that, when we do the mudras of the Devi or any Devata, female deity or male deity, we become that deity. And it has been my unfailing experience that the moment I do the mudras, something happens. You could say it is purely psychological, but my whole consciousness elevates to a different level; I experience a different flow of energy in my body.

In Gayatri sadhana, there are two sets of mudras. One set of 24 mudras is performed before the chanting is done, and 8 mudras are done after the chanting. The 24 preliminary mudras are *samukham*, *samputam*, *vitatam*, *vistratam*, *dvimukham*, *trimukham*, *chaturmukham*, *panchmukham*, *shanmukham*, *adhomukham*, *vyapakanjalim*, *shakatam*, *yamapasham*, *granthim*, *unmukhonmukham*, *pralambam*, *mushtikam, matasya, kurma, varahkam, simhakrantam, mahakrantam, mudgaram* and *pallavam.*

I've explained these mudras with pictures in the appendix.

Step Twenty-Three

Upcharas are devotional offerings. You can make 16 or 5 offerings. Offerings are usually made of water, a little honey, some rice and other such ingredients, but if you want to keep it pure, and if you don't have anything for an offering, you can just do an offering mentally. When I was in the woods, there was no way I could offer all these ingredients to Mother Divine. Sourcing them would have been difficult and even if I could have sourced them, the rats would have eaten them anyway, so I did the offerings mentally.

The usual convention is to add "Om" at the beginning followed by the name of the ingredient and then "*samarpyami*" in the end. *Samarpyami* means "I'm offering this to you". For example, if you are offering incense to the deity, just say, "*Om dhoopam smarpyami.*" *Panchaopchara* – five offerings – is normally the least you can do. The conventional five offerings are:

Dhoopam (incense), *deepam* (lamp), *naivaedyam* (anything edible like a sweetmeat, a fruit, etc. It can also be a plate full of food), *tambulam* (betel leaves) and *pungiphalam* (*supari* – commonly known as betel nut or areca nut). So while offering these, your mantras will become:

Om dhoopam samarpyami
Om deepam darshyami

(Here "*darshyami*" is used rather than "*samarpyami*" to indicate that "I'm showing the lamp", as opposed to "offering the lamp").

Om naivedyam samarpyami
Om tambulam samarpyami
Om pungiphalam samarpyami

When you make mental offerings, you can simply say, "*Om dhoopam, deepam, naivedyam, tambulam, pungiphalam samarpyami.*"

Step Twenty-Four

In this step, we perform mantra *samskara*. There is no real equivalent of the word *samskara* in English. Broadly translated, it could mean cultural values, upbringing or an act marking transformation. In Sanatana Dharma, there are 16 *samskaras*, important milestones, in the life of a human being that mark the beginning of a new chapter in a person's life. The same courtesy is extended to the living energy of any mantra we invoke. Gayatri is no exception.

The mantra of Gayatri was cursed by Brahma, Vasishtha and Vishwamitra. So the primary *samskara* of Gayatri mantra is to absolve it from the curse of the sages (*shaap vimochana*). To do so, chant the *shaap vimochana* mantra of Brahma, Vasishtha and Vishwamitra seven times each. If you cannot do seven times each, doing it thrice each will also do, but that's the bare minimum. The mantras are provided in the appendix.

Please note that this book is written for those who are not initiated. If you are initiated into Gayatri mantra, you only have to do mantra *samskara* based on what your guru tells you. Usually, it's done only on the first day – sometimes not even on the first day, but before the beginning of the sadhana. If you are not initiated into the Gayatri mantra, you'd have to do it every day.

Step Twenty-Five

The 25th step is mantra *dhayanam*. Now sometimes, in some sadhanas you have what we call a *dhyana shloka,* which is usually a verse that depicts the Devi – that talks about how your object of worship looks, what implements she carries, what kind of face she has, her physical appearance – so you can meditate on that form. If you want to keep it very simple, just chant your Gayatri mantra and let that be your *dhyan shloka*. Or you can go online, where you can find a myriad of images of Vedmata Gayatri. Pick the one that appeals to you, and meditate on that form in the beginning. If you are keen on using on the *dhyana shloka*, I've provided that in the appendix.

Step Twenty-Six

Now the good news: you are ready to do the chanting, *mool mantra japa*, step number 26, where you will pick up your beads and start chanting. You will chant based on the *sankalpa* you have taken, so if you had said, "I am going to chant 'x' number of times a day," that's what you will do. If you had said, "I'm only going to chant 'x' number of minutes a day," then that's what you will do.

I would like to remind you that consistency in chanting is extremely important.

Step Twenty-Seven

Once you have done the chanting, we show *uttara* mudra or post-*japa* handlocks. A couple of them may seem a bit complicated, but they aren't. Eight handlocks are shown in this step. They are *dhenu*, *gyanam*, *vairagya*, *yoni*, *shankha*, *pankaja*, *samhara*, *lingam* and *nirvana* mudra (also known as *samhara* mudra).

In the olden days, teachers would make their students slog for years before they would teach mudras. Sometimes, a disciple would train for 12 years, yet the teacher would not instruct them on mudras at all. When we get something after much time, effort and energy, we usually value it. I have given you the mudras freely, but please don't think that these mudras are casual gestures. Mudras represent a powerful method to aid the flow of energy.

Once you have done these, you just do the *namaste* mudra also known as *anjali* mudra. It is done in the standard *namaste* posture by joining both hands and bringing them to your chest.

Step Twenty-Eight

This step is called *japa samarpana* which means offering your chanting you just did. We have to offer the *japa* back to the deity we have been praying to, because we haven't done this *japa* for us but for the welfare of all sentient beings. This higher sense of consciousness is required so you don't just feel like you have become the object of your worship but also behave like one in the truest sense of the word.

I don't deny that whenever most of us do *sadhana*, we do it because somehow we want to benefit from it. Yes, I as an individual want to benefit from my chanting, but remember that at a soul level, we are all interconnected. The more you flourish, the more I will gain – that's the precept under which we function. The more everybody is enjoying themselves, the more I will enjoy myself.

There was once a farmer who had a cornfield, and every year he would distribute free seeds to all his neighbors. One day, his friends said to him, "Why do you spend so much money every year distributing free seeds? People never give you anything in return."

"I do that because it benefits me."

"How can it benefit you?"

"You see," he replied, "when birds, bees and other insects carry pollen, they will always carry pollen from adjoining fields. If the fields around me have healthy corn, then the corn in my field is also going to be good, but if the corn in the fields around me is unhealthy, if it is infested with pests and so on, then I would also be affected. So, it is in my best interest to ensure that the farmers around me get good produce. When I give them good seeds, it helps me directly."

In other words, we are all affected by karmic cross-pollination.

Most of our actions are usually performed for selfish reasons, that everything is geared towards my happiness, my fulfillment, my desires, my goals and my ambitions. This one karma of chanting, of calling out to the Divine, let this not be for me. For once, let me understand that this is for the welfare of all sentient beings, because if they are going to benefit from my actions, then clearly, I will benefit too.

With that in mind, we visualize the deity, Vedmata Gayatri. Mentally offer your chanting in the left hand of Devi. Visualize that Devi, Mother Gayatri, Mother Divine is there, and you have offered it in the left hand of Devi. You can simply say, "I hereby offer you all my *japa*." It's as if you are a child who has earned something, and are giving it to your parents for safekeeping – "Please, put it in a fixed deposit," or the like. Now, chant,

Abhishta siddhim me dehi
sharanagata vatsale bhaktya
samarpaye tubhyam
japamevarcanam

That, "O Devi, I have done this *japa* with a pure intention; let that intention manifest. I am offering you all my *japa*." In this way, you very smartly reinforce why you did the *japa* in the first place, and you have devoted all your *japa* to your deity. This is a crucial step. I always tell those whom I initiate that if you miss this step, your *purushcharana* is *khandit* – it's broken.

One way to ensure that you remember this step is to

make notes (one of my personal practices: I always make notes.) I don't rely entirely on my memory. I have a small list where I write down step one, step two, step three, etcetera. And I always have that list sitting beside me during my sadhana. If you do your *japa* correctly, you may enter a different state of consciousness, and you may forget a step or two. Under those circumstances, it is important to have the steps of your *japa* written down.

Once you have devoted your *japa* to your deity, you can then pray for everybody's welfare. There is a little *shloka*, a little mantra, which is, "*Sarve bhavantu sukhina, sarve santu niramaya, sarve Bhadrani paschyanti, maa kaschida dukha bhaga bhavet.*" In case you can't remember this, just pray, with your hands folded, "May everybody be at peace in this beautiful world."

Step Twenty-Nine

Now, it's time to free all the energies you may have invoked during your *japa*. I have simplified the Gayatri sadhana so we are not invoking so many energies. In advanced mantra sadhanas, you invite many different kinds of energies to be there while you are doing your *japa*, because you are inviting Devi, and you would not want to invite Her on Her own. Freeing all the energies is called *visarjana*, so we gratefully and gracefully see them off, and they can go where they wish. You can simply fold your hands and say, "Thank you very much, whoever came here, please be with me next time," or you can chant this simple *shloka*:

Gaccha gaccha param sthanam svasthanam paramesvari,
pujaradhanakale ca punaragamanaya ca.

May you all return to your abode, I humbly request you to please be here, when I call upon you once again to offer my prayers to you.

Tistha Tistha Parasthane Svasthane Paramesvari,
Yatra brahmadayo devah sarve tisthanti me hrdi ||

Let everybody go to your abode and be settled there.

May all the positive energies, all the goodness, forever remain in my heart. Let those I need not go from here.

There are energies that simply help you fulfill your material goals, but then there are energies that are part of your purification that should remain with you to help you progress on the spiritual path. Let those positive energies stay inside me, in my heart – that's what this verse means.

Step Thirty

Step number 30 is to say sorry for any mistakes you might have made while chanting, whether that's yawning, losing focus, feeling angry or negative or even thinking ill of people, and so on. These are all errors of commission – you know they have been committed. Seeking forgiveness is imperative, so we do a little *kshama prarthana*, a request for pardon and once again, you can either read the translation on page 186 or you can just say sorry in any language and words that you feel comfortable with. Or you can just chant this little *stotra* that I have given on page 196 of the book:

Aparadhasahastrani kriyantesharnisam maya,
Dasosyamiti mam matva ksamasva paramesrvari.
Avahanam na janami na janami visarjanam,
Pujam caiva na janami ksamyatam paramesrvari.
Mantrahinam kriyahinam bhaktihinam suresrvari,
Yatpujitam maya devi paripurna tadastu me.

This means that I have made countless mistakes, please look upon me as Your humble servant and forgive me. I don't know the mantras, I don't know the correct pronunciation, I am an ignorant person, and yet I have the audacity to pray to You because You are ever merciful, You still fulfill my wishes.

Step Thirty-One

Now it's time to perform *yajna*, fire offerings. The ten-percent principle (*dashansh*) applies here. Which means, if you have chanted 3000 times, you will make 300 fire offerings. Once again, I've given a chapter on fire offerings in the appendix.

There are many ways to do elaborate *yajnas*, but perhaps perform the simplest one. There is not much to be done. If you cannot do fire offerings, simply double the number of chants. For example, if you chanted 1000 times that day, this means you would make 100 oblations to the fire. If you cannot do a *yajna*, simply chant an additional 200 times, over and above your 1000 mantra chanting, to compensate for not doing the *yajna.*

One essential point on fire offerings: Whenever you offer anything to the fire of the *yagna,* make sure you end it with the words '*Om svaha*'.

For example, to make a fire offering with Gayatri mantra, you will say,

> *"Om Bhurbhuvah Svaha Tatsaviturvarenyama Bhargo Devasya, Dhimahi, Dhiyo Yo Nah Pracodayata, Om Svaha."*

Step Thirty-Two

After the *yajna,* we do *tarpan* or libations. There are many kinds of *tarpan* – *Brahma tarpan, pitra tarpan, deva tarpan* and so on. The *tarpan* we are doing here is *deva tarpan,* that we are offering to the deity. When you offer somebody food, you offer her some water as well, because water completes the meal. I am telling you the simplest method of *tarpan.*

It can be done with water mixed with sesame seeds and so on, but this simple *tarpan* is done with just water. You can use that little pot that you had to do *achamana,* and complete the libation in either of two ways: You can take some water from the pot with a little spoon and as you chant your mantra, "*Om bhurbhuvah svah tatsaviturvarenayama bhargo devasya dhimahi dhiyo yo nah pracodayata, Om tarpayami.*"

Like we append "*Om svaha*" in a fire offering, we add, "*Om tarpyami*" while performing libations.

This is the recommended method. If you don't have a spoon you can join your ring finger and thumb and dip them in the pot. The number of libations is always ten percent of your fire offerings. So, if you did 1000 times chanting, you'll make 100 fire offerings and 10 libations.

Step Thirty-Three

At this point comes *marjanam* or *abhishekam*, which is like a coronation. The idea is that now that you have performed the mantra and the associated ceremonies, when you walk out into the real world, you don't want to operate like a normal human being – you want to be divine; you want to be like your object of worship. Coronation *or marjanam* is done in the belief that you are a *devata* now. You have done *nyasa* earlier, you have placed the letters, you have done the mudras, you have done the chanting, you have invoked the energy, you are in Devi *bhava* – you have requested the energy to stay inside you, and now you are that energy.

With that feeling, you do *marjanam*, which is usually one-tenth of libations. So if you have done 1000 *japa*, you would do one-hundred fire offerings; *tarpan* would be done ten times, and *marjanam* only once. Alternatively, you could base your sadhana on time, as I did. I would sit down for ten hours for my *japa*; I would do *yagna* for one hour, *tarpan* for six minutes – and then another three minutes or so of *marjanam*, rather than one-tenth of six minutes, which would run into mere seconds. Note that the *japa* has to be the same factor every day, but the last count, for *marjanam*, can be in round figures.

Be mindful that the water for *tarpan* cannot be used for *marjanam.* It would be like reusing somebody's old bathwater. That's not a nice image but it's something like that.

To do *marjanam*, have some water in a little pot, join your ring finger with your thumb, dip it in the pot and then sprinkle it over your head with the still-joined ring finger and thumb. Add "*Om marjayami*" at the end. So, it becomes:

> *"Om bhurbhuvah svah tatsaviturvarenayama bhargo devasya dhimahi dhiyo yo nah pracodayata, Om marjayami."*

You sprinkle the water on your head after saying the mantra above.

Now you have crowned yourself with that energy, you are free to roam around fearlessly like a king in the world. As it says in *Devi Apradha Kshama Stotra*:

> *Shvapako jalpako bhavti madhupakomagira*
> *Niratanko ranko viharati chiram kotikanakaih*
> *Tavaparne karne vishati manvarne phalamidam*
> *Janah ko janeete janani japaneeyam japvidhhau*

Oh Mother, the one who possesses no attraction of speech, the one who has no wisdom becomes all-attractive and very wise. Even a beggar becomes king and roams fearlessly. This is the result, if even a tiny bit of the devotion, even one letter of Your mantra reaches somebody's ears. If someone was to do Your entire sadhana properly, who knows what that person will be blessed with.

You have done *abhishekam, marjanam,* and you are walking around with that energy. It will elevate you. You will feel greater self-esteem; you will feel stronger. You will feel, "I don't need so much external approval. I don't need other people. I can make my own way – I can breeze over hurdles and cut through obstacles," and so on.

Step Thirty-Four

This step is about charity, which is an integral part of a good sadhana. It's also called *sadhaka bhojan* or Brahmin *bhojan.* In this, we usually gather some people and feed them. It is a moment of celebration as well as expressing your gratitude.

Sadhaka bhojan is usually one-tenth of the coronation process. For example, if you have done a 1,00,000 *japa*, let's say in 40 days, then the total fire offerings would be 10,000, *tarpan* would be 1000, *marjanam* would be 100 and you would feed 10 people. Over the course of 40 days, this is usually done on the final day. You could also do it daily. For example, when I was in the woods during my sadhana, I used to set aside some money every day with the intention that I would just give it to somebody or feed some people at the end of my *purushcharana.*

Until we do sadhaka *bhojan*, everything we have done is for abstract energy; for some deity. But when we feed people, we are feeding the living God: we are feeding the energy that is living in other people – they talk, bathe, walk, sleep, eat and so on – that gives the proof that we exist; that the soul which is there in every living entity exists.

When the soul leaves the body, you are declared dead. You may be a billionaire or a very learned person – whatever you have been, when you are deceased, we say, "He or she is dead now." Nothing lives on. Your legacy is only your good karma. Everything else dies, so feeding other people express our gratitude to those around us.

Step Thirty-Five

After you have fed people, you need to seek forgiveness again. You can repeat the small prayer outlined in step number 30 or just express your sentiments in any language. Even something as simple as, "Thank you for coming. I seek your forgiveness for any shortcomings, and so on," will do.

There was a young boy who went to his friend's place for dinner. His friend's mother cooked the food and brought it to the table. When she served it, the boy started eating straightaway.

"Oh, don't you say grace before you eat food?" the hosts said. "Don't you pray to God?"

"I don't have to," he replied, "my mum cooks very good food."

The danger is that when you accumulate energy, you move towards a sense of invincibility. And when that happens, it can get to one's head very quickly. That is the beginning of the downfall of a good *sadhaka*. The idea behind all this is that we should remain humble; we should remain grounded.

Step Thirty-Six

If there's any water left in any of the pots from your sadhana, *yajna*, *tarpan*, etc., you can now offer it to the sun – just face the sun and pour the water in front of you. The notion here is that if you're facing the sun, the sun's rays are falling on you; there is some heat, which means if you put some water on the ground, part of it is going to evaporate and help distant entities. Part of it is going to be absorbed by the earth and is going to help many other organisms. If you are living in a country where there is snow or inclement weather or you can't step out for any reason, you can pour the water in a flower pot or at the root of some plant or tree, so that it is not wasted.

This concludes the comprehensive method of 36 steps.

The Brief Invocation

At the beginning of this chapter, I shared with you that if you are pressed for time, you can choose the brief method of invocation. If your sentiment is true and your intentions well-placed, you will surely benefit just as much from brief invocation, which has 7 steps.

The only thing to bear in mind is that if you undertake a *purushcharana* using the brief method then that's the method you must continue with throughout your sadhana. In other words, if you vow to chant over 40 days and begin it with the comprehensive method of 36 steps, you can't move to just the brief one on day two.

In addition to the three steps of *sankalpa* (step number 16, which is additional and has to be done only on the first day), and steps 1 and 2 which are bathing and putting on fresh clothes, here are the 7 steps of brief invocation:

1. Purification of the surroundings (Step 4). Just sprinkle water in all directions.
2. Self-purification (Step 5). Drink water three times.
3. Lighting the lamp (Step 6). You can do it without chanting any mantra.
4. Ganesha prayer (Step 7). Once again, you can do it without mudra or any specific mantra.
5. Mantra chanting (Step 26). Chant as per your *sankalpa*.
6. Offering *japa* to the deity (Step 28). This is *japa samarpana*.
7. Seeking forgiveness (Step 30). You can either chant the *stotra* given in step 30 earlier or you can simply seek forgiveness for any mistakes or errors.

With this, we have covered all the steps of Gayatri sadhana. Now you know everything there is to know about the Gayatri mantra.

In the olden days, when there was only oral transmission of information, and even when there was the written word, the knowledge I have given you was reserved for ascetics or Brahmins. We are done with this ignorance; we don't need this anymore. After thousands of years of divisive policies, we need to move towards unification. This has hurt our country for far too long and certainly in spiritual activities, it is not at all needed. Everybody is entitled to all the wisdom that is there, and it's up to people how much of it they use it for themselves.

I have not held anything back and has shared everything without any discrimination whatsoever. If Kaushika can become Vishwamitra, a *Brahmarishi,* then each of us can rise above this conditioning.

The Story of Kalavati

When I was small, there was a woman who lived at the far end of our street with her four children. Her name was Kalavati, and she was illiterate. Her husband had held a government job, but he died when her eldest daughter was about seven years old. There was a provision in her husband's department that in case an employee died while still in service, someone from the family would get a job in their place. But with Kalavati being illiterate and children small, none of them could get a job. She took to washing dishes and cleaning people's homes, which was the only work she could do to feed her family. Kalavati had great faith in Shiva, and there was only one mantra that she chanted all the time: *Om Namah Shivaya*. This simple mantra was the mantra of her life.

I was quite young, not even four years old, when Kalavati was widowed. It did not even occur to me she might have had a husband at some point in time. I thought she had always been that way, just her with four children, doing dishes in people's homes.

My mother said to her once, "I cannot allow you to do dishes in my home because you are a very spiritual person, and I cannot live with the burden that you will do dishes and clean homes. So I will just pay you something – we'll get somebody else to do the work."

Over the years, something remarkable happened to Kalavati. Her face started to shine like the sun. She was the first person whom I saw who had not just a soft glow to her skin, but a radiance so striking, as if it was just flowing from her – and she was somebody who did not even have money to buy soap. Her heels were badly cracked too, because she could not afford slippers – any time somebody gifted her slippers, she would simply give them to one of her daughters or sons. She would say, "My children need slippers more than I do." So her heels were cracked, but her face glowed mightily.

By the time she turned sixty, not even one wrinkle formed on her skin. There was just her large, glowing face, with her giant forehead framed by matted locks, because she was very poor.

At first, she and her children lived in only one room. With some help, they managed to get another room for two of her children, then one of her sons got married and the other one started riding a little rickshaw. She put a tin roof over them, and that's where she would live. In that little place, there was a bed and a large picture of Shiva, and she would spend all of her time there.

One day, when my parents were looking for a match for my sister, she came to our home and said to my sister, "Tomorrow, some people are coming to see you." My mother was there, as was I. I was now 16 years old. We were all surprised, because indeed someone was coming to see if there was a possibility of a marital alliance, but we hadn't told anybody. Kalavati said, "They will come in a white car, high car. The boy will be wearing a shirt with stripes." And for some reason, she added, "They will end up staying longer than planned. And you will get married here. "And oh," she said, "The boy is fair-skinned."

The next day, some people showed up in a white Tata Sierra – a boy with a fair complexion, along with his mother and sister. He was wearing a shirt with stripes. Can you imagine? And he accidentally locked his ignition key in the car, which delayed them. They called somebody to help, but they couldn't open the door lock. Finally, they broke the window of the car so they could get into it. Everything she said came to pass, word for word, except that my sister never got married there. And the alliance never actually happened.

There was a funny reason for that.

When they had to break the window of the car, the mother of the prospective groom became concerned. She was a widow from a very well off family, and had been through a good deal of suffering in her life. She thought the episode with the window to be a bad omen. "I am worried," she said. "If this is what is happening before the wedding, then afterwards, God knows what all we will have to bear."

When you chant a mantra with devotion and faith, you develop very sharp intuition – but that does not mean everything you say will come true. It can, provided you remain emotionally unattached. Kalavati loved our family, she came on her own volition to make those predictions, and she wanted my sister to get married there.

Herein lies two of your greatest challenges as a *sadhak*: a) To not say things that are not part of your intuition, and b) To know what isn't part of your intuition. You must ask yourself, is what I am saying coloured by my emotions? For example, you might say to someone, "Don't worry, everything is going to work out." Are you saying this because you care about that person and you don't want him to go through any trouble, or are you saying this because you are hearing, feeling or perceiving it that way?

When you do mudras and when you do *nyasa* correctly, the chances of such errors lessen significantly, because you are in Devi *bhava* – you are in the sentiment of your deity. You are unlikely to just blabber out of a sense of attachment; to say things that you want to happen. Instead, you would say things objectively, like a radiologist reading a report or scan. There comes a discerning wisdom when you chant a mantra correctly.

It will also reinforce your faith. Kalavati's daughter got married, and was later was burned for dowry. She received third-degree burns and the moment Kalavati heard the news, she came running to my mother and said, "Look what has happened." Kalavati was scared because being unlettered she thought how would she talk to the doctors, which hospital, what ward, how would she get the medicines from the pharmacist and so on. Her daughter was in a different city and Matarani (my mother) told her, "Don't worry, we will take care of her." Matarani took some of her own money, and collected some funds from two of her colleagues, Reeta and Veena. With this, Kalavati's daughter's treatment was done, and she was saved with God's grace.

During this extraordinarily painful event, Kalavati never questioned her faith, never faltered. She was very graceful. She just said to my mother, "I cannot see my daughter in this state." Not once did she say, "Why me, Shiva, why me, Lord? Why my daughter? I have been praying to you all my life and here my daughter is, burnt by her husband. Why? Is this the reward of faith?" This is what a beggar or a trader does – one who is doing *bhakti* like a business transaction: I have done this for God, now God will be pleased with me, therefore, nothing bad should happen to me. Kalavati was made of different material. She and her faith were unwavering.

Some more time passed. She came to me once, and said, "Very soon, you will go abroad." In a matter of months, I was in Australia. She also used to consult me, by the way. I am only telling you one half of the story. For astrology and the like, she had many a good conversation with me. She would drop by, and it always gave me great joy to serve her – to feed her, to give her some gift, which she often refused. It doesn't matter who you are – somehow, when somebody is truly spiritual, sooner or later you experience that person's goodness.

Kalavati was proof that you chant a mantra to purify yourself, to be more spiritual. It doesn't matter how much of a believer or non-believer you are; how staunch an atheist you are – sooner or later, faith will take its place in your heart, as if it owns it, which it does.

The first time I came back from Australia in December 2000, I went and met Kalavati. She was living in the same old, run-down place. I said to her, "You shouldn't be living under this tin roof. Please allow me to build a decent home for you. You can have your own washroom." There was a little space there, and I said, "We can manage something here. You can even have your own air conditioner."

"No, no, I don't want an air conditioner," she said. "My children would not let me have it. Besides, who is going to pay the electricity bill?"

"At least let me get you a water cooler. I can take care of the electricity bill."

"No, I don't want it. I won't live here."

"The best I can do, then," I said, "is to give you the money and you can build whenever you wish."

"Okay," she said, "I will let you know." But a year passed, and she did not take up my offer. I called my mother, and said, "I promised her something, but she wouldn't take the money at that time, and the room is still not built. I've given my word; I've made a pledge, and I want to fulfill it. So I am sending you the money – just give it to her: Say, "Put it in the river, I don't care. But you have to do something with it."

At my mother's bidding, Kalavati finally accepted. I went to meet her on my next visit again. And I remember, when I bowed for her blessings, she gave me a hard slap on my back, because she was in her *bhava*. She would never do that to anybody, for the record. She said. "Sit," and made me sit. She chanted her mantra and came into her sentiment. Her body started shaking a little, and then she gave me a solid blow on my back with her palm again. At that time, I felt I had been given something special. You know how sometimes you have an experience that only you can comprehend, and is almost impossible to describe? And at that moment, I felt all those years that I'd been doing Shiva's chant – I used to do many kinds of Shiva sadhanas – I had received the fruit of it all.

Soon afterwards, Kalavati stopped cleaning people's homes. She ceased working altogether; she would just remain in that one room, chanting all day and all night. That was her life, and with each passing day, she looked younger. I have hardly seen such a glow on anyone's face, as I have with hers. The radiance seemed to shine from within her skin, and under her matted locks, her face was utterly beautiful – to that, I am a witness.

Without any pain, or suffering in her last days, she slipped quietly into the other world.

This is what mantras can do when you chant them with reverence.

There comes a time when you go beyond the Vedas and all kinds of *tapas*. Firmly established in your devotional sentiment, you become one with the Divine, says Krishna in the *Bhagavad Gita.** Besides, he says, the one who has

---

* *vedeṣhu yajñeṣhu tapaḥsu chaiva dāneṣhu yat puṇya-phalaṁ pradiṣhṭam, atyeti tat sarvam idaṁ viditvā yogī paraṁ sthānam upaiti chādyam. The Bhagavad Gita, 8.28.* Yogis who know the secret of leaving this world peacefully (Krishna expounds in the earlier verses) go beyond the merit gained from the Vedic rituals, austerities, sacrifices and so on. They merge in the Supreme Consciousness.

found a vast lake of fresh water no longer has any need of small springs here and there. Such becomes the state of one whom has surrendered to the Divine Will.*

The glow on Kalavati's face was not just out of sadhana, it was of *bhakti* and goodness. She was completely illiterate, and picked the simplest mantra, because that's the mantra her guru had given her. She would go and see her guru once in four or five years, because she did not have the money or the time to travel; she did not do her guru's *darshan* more than five or six times in her entire life. But she never stopped chanting that mantra. *Om Namah Shivaya* was not what she uttered – it was what she had become. That's the power of sound, of devotion, faith, of mantras.

To do my job properly, I have shared with you everything that I have done or known about Gayatri sadhana, now it is up to you to take it forward in your own life. Based on your temperament, mindset, circumstances, lifestyle and so on, you can choose what appeals to you. Be patient. As associating with a trained singer or a concert pianist does not make you an expert musician, simply reading my books or getting initiation from me won't do much at all. At the end of the day, it is your own practice alone that will help you sail across.

---

* The full verse is *yāvān artha udapāne sarvataḥ samplutodake, tāvānsarveṣhu vedeṣhu brāhmaṇasya vijānataḥ. The Bhagavad Gita, 2.46.* It also means that a large source of water can serve the same purpose as many small sources of water. Similarly, many small pleasures of the material world are automatically fulfilled for the one who realizes the Supreme Truth.

I can only do two things, both of which I do sincerely, to the best of my abilities. One, share with you all that I know. Two, pray for you.

I offer this work to you.

APPENDIX

In this section:

1. Gayatri Sadhana with 36 steps with transliteration and translation for quick reference while you do the sadhana
2. Arrangement of pots
3. How to make fire offerings

Sadhana Steps - The Comprehensive Method

1. Bathe

Chant the following mantra while putting the first mug of water on you (or when you step into the shower, if you are taking a shower):

Sanskrit (Devanagari)	*Sanskrit (IAST)*
गंगा च यमुने चैव गोदावरी सरस्वती | नर्मदे सिंधु कावेरी जलेस्मिन संनिधिम कुरु ||	Gaṃgā ca Yamune caiva Godāvarī Sarasvatī | Narmade Siṃdhu Kāverī jalesmina saṃnidhima kuru ||
Translation	
I invoke the holy presence of Ganga, Yamuna, Godavari, Saraswati, Narmada, Sindhu and Kaveri in this water.	

2. Put on fresh clothes

3. Enter the sanctum sanctorum or open your altar

Gently tap on the floor with your left heel and say out loud, "*Om Hrim Astraya Phat!*"

4. Purification

Once inside the pooja *griha*, you begin by purifying yourself and the energies around you. Use your left hand to take a bit of water using the spoon in your vessel and put it in the right one. Chant the following mantra:

Om apavitrah pavitro vā
Sarvāvasthāṁ gato api vā
Yaḥ smaret puṇḍarīkākṣaṁ
Sa bahya abhyantaraṁ śuciḥ

Sprinkle the water in your hand above and around you.

5. Self-Purification (*Achamana*)

Water is consecrated and drunk three times while performing *achamana*. It's done three times to purify you at the emotional, mental and physical level. To purify you in your waking, sleeping and dreaming state. To purify the three modes of material nature, that is, goodness, passion and ignorance. To infuse you with knowledge, existence, bliss (*sat-chit-anand*). To ignite your potential, kinetic and creative energies.

With your left hand, using the spoon again, put some water in your right hand and say the following mantra:

Om Keshvaya Namah

Drink the water.
Put one more spoon and say the following mantra.

Om Madhavaya Namah

Drink the water.
One more spoon and say the following mantra:

Om Narayanaya Namaha

Drink the holy water.

5b. *Prakshalana*

Once you have done the *achamana* three times, take some more water in your right hand (a spoonful is usually enough) and symbolically wash both your hands while saying the following mantra:

Om Pundarikakshaya Namah

6. Light the lamp

You can simply use your guru mantra while lighting the lamp or chant the following mantra:

Om agni jyotir jyotir agnih swaha
Suryo jyoti jyotir suryah swaha
Agnir varcho jyotir varchah swaha
Suryo varcho jyotir varchah swaha
Jyoti suryah suryo jyotih swaha

(May the divine energy bring the power of Agni in this lamp. The light of this lamp is Agni, and Agni is this lamp... *Svaha*, let all afflictions burn.)

7. Invoke Ganesha (Ganesh *Dhyana*)

You can pray to Lord Ganesha either by any mantra you may already know or by folding your hands and reciting any or both the mantras given below:

Sanskrit (Devanagari)	*Sanskrit (IAST)*
वक्रतुण्ड महाकाय सूर्यकोटि समप्रभ । निर्विघ्नं कुरु मे देव सर्वकार्येषु सर्वदा ॥	Vakratuṇḍa mahākāya sūryakoṭi samaprabha । Nirvighnaṃ kuru me deva sarvakāryeṣu sarvadā ॥
Translation	
O Lord Ganesha of curved trunk, magnificent body exuding the radiance of countless suns, please be by my side and help me complete my task.	

Sanskrit (Devanagari)	*Sanskrit (IAST)*
सुमुखश्च-एकदंतश्च कपिलो गज कर्णक: लम्बोदरश्व विकटो विघ्ननाशो विनायक: धूम्रकेतुर्गणाध्यक्षो भालचन्द्रो गजानन:	Sumukhaśca-ekadaṃtaśca kapilo gaja karṇaka: Lambodaraśva vikaṭo vighnanāśo vināyaka: Dhūmraketurgaṇādhyakṣo bhālacandro gajānana:

Sanskrit (Devanagari)	*Sanskrit (IAST)*
द्वादशैतानि नामानि य: पठेच्छर्णुयादपि विद्यारम्भे विवाहे च प्रवेशे निर्गमे तथा संग्रामें संकटे चैव विघ्नस्तस्य न जयते।	Dvādaśaitāni nāmāni ya: paṭheccharṇuyādapi Vidyārambhe vivāhe ca praveśe nirgame tathā Saṃgrāmeṃ saṃkaṭe caiva vighnastasya na jayate I
Translation	
O Ganesha of beautiful face, one tusk, crimson red and elephant ears. O beautiful pot-bellied Ganesha who is hard on enemies, slayer of obstacles and a great spiritual preceptor. O Ganesha who is sometimes the color of smoke, the chief of ganas, who sports a moon on his forehead and walks like an elephant, whoever chants these twelve names of yours before studying, marrying, entering a new home, in battlefield, in distress (or embarking on any important journey of their lives) is sure to receive your help.	

8. Handlocks for Ganesha (Ganesh Mudra)

Show the three mudras of Ganesha.

First mudra of Ganesha:

a. Bring your left hand closer to your chest with the back of your hand facing your chest.
b. Curl your left hand a little and grab it with your right hand to form the mudra below.

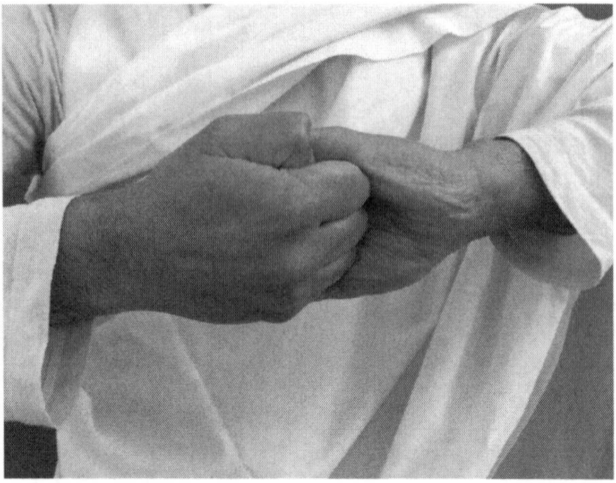

Second mudra of Ganesha:

a. Tuck the index and ring fingers of your left hand in your right fist.
b. Let the middle finger of your left hand remain outside to form the trunk of Ganesha.
c. Slightly protrude the thumb and little finger of your left hand to form the ears of Ganesha.

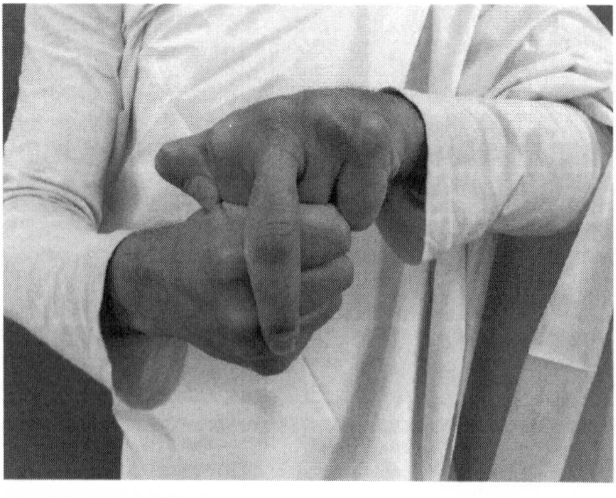

Third mudra of Ganesha:

It's exactly the same as the second mudra, just that Ganesha is made with the right hand.

d. Tuck the index and ring fingers of your right hand in your left fist.
e. Let the middle finger of your right hand remain outside to form the trunk of Ganesha.
f. Slightly protrude the thumb and little finger of your right hand to form the ears of Ganesh as per the image below.

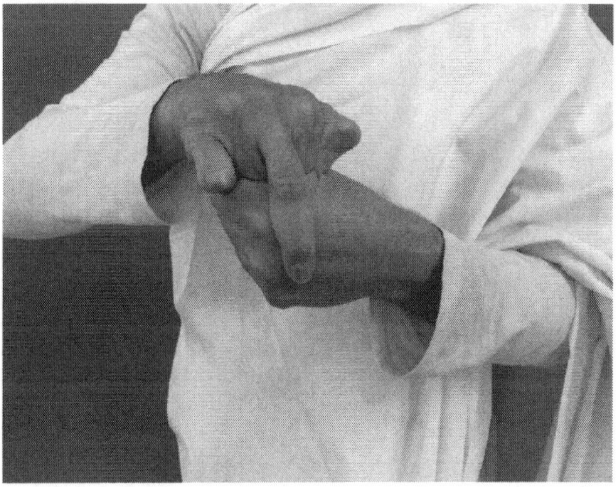

9. Chant the hymn of auspiciousness (*Svastivachana*)

A chant to invite and invoke the Vedic energies around you is done at this stage. It is usually done by chanting a specific hymn called *Svastivachana*. You can either chant the *Svastivachana* or just the following verses taken from the *Rigveda* (1.89.8):

Sanskrit (Devanagari)	*Sanskrit (IAST)*
ॐ भद्रं कर्णेभिः शृणुयाम देवाः ।	Oṃ bhadraṃ karṇebhiḥ śṛṇuyāma devāḥ |
भद्रं पश्येमाक्षभिर्यजत्राः	Bhadraṃ paśyemākṣabhirya jatrāḥ
स्थिरैरङ्गैस्तुष्टुवागँसस्तनूभिः	Sthirairaṅgaistuṣṭuvāgam sastanūbhiḥ
व्यशेम देवहितं यदायूः	Vyaśema devahitaṃ yadāyūḥ
स्वस्ति न इन्द्रो वृद्धश्रवाः	Svasti na indro vṛddhaśravāḥ
स्वस्ति नः पूषा विश्ववेदाः	Svasti naḥ pūṣā viśvavedāḥ
स्वस्ति नस्ताक्षर्यो अरिष्टनेमिः	Svasti nastākṣaryo ariṣṭanemiḥ
स्वस्ति नो ब्रुहस्पतिर्दधातु ।	Svasti no bruhaspatirdadhātu |
ॐ शान्तिः शान्तिः शान्तिः	Oṃ śāntiḥ śāntiḥ śāntiḥ

Translation
May we only hear auspicious sounds with our ears and may only see divine things with our eyes. May we lead a stable life of health and prosperity with gratitude throughout the lifespan granted to us. May Indra of great renown protect us. May the omniscient Poosha protect us. May Lord Garuda destroy all harm and negativity. May Brihaspati protect us.

10. Meditate on your guru (Guru *dhyana*)

Now that you have purified yourself and the environment around you by invoking various energies, it is time to meditate on your guru. Call upon your guru by offering a flower if you have your guru's picture or you can simply visualize your guru's form and chant the following mantra with reverence:

Sanskrit (Devanagari)	*Sanskrit (IAST)*
गुरुर्ब्रह्मा गुरुर्विष्णुर्गुरुर्देवो महेश्वरः ।	Gururbrahmā gururviṣṇurgururdevo maheśvaraḥ ।
गुरुरेव परं ब्रह्म तस्मै श्रीगुरवे नमः ॥	Gurureva paraṃ brahma tasmai śrīgurave namaḥ ॥
Translation	
Guru is Brahma, guru is Vishnu, guru is Shiva himself. Guru is verily Para-Brahma (Supreme Soul). Humble obeisance and salutations to my guru.	

11. Chant the guru mantra (Guru mantra *japa*)

Now you should chant your guru mantra 11, 21 or 108 times depending on either the routine given to you by your guru or your own usual routine.

12. Obeisance to all *siddhas*

Offer your respects and gratitude to all the *siddhas*, sages, seers and gurus of the past. Generally, this mantra can differ from tradition to tradition but if your guru is not a mantra adept (therefore not knowing this mantra) or hasn't initiated you into this mantra. Simply chant the following:

Sanskrit (Devanagari)	*Sanskrit (IAST)*	*Translation*
ॐ दिव्यौघ नमः	Oṃ divyaugha namaḥ	My obeisance to all the *siddhas* of divine bodies.
ॐ सिद्धौघ नमः	Oṃ siddhaugha namaḥ	My obeisance to all the *siddhas* of the past who are no more in their physical bodies.
ॐ मानवौघ नमः	Oṃ mānavaugha namaḥ	My obeisance to all the *siddhas* who are either still in a human body or can assume one.

13. Meditating on your deity (*Ishta dhyana*)

Sanskrit (Devanagari)	*Sanskrit (IAST)*
ॐ बालां विद्यां तु गायत्रीं लोहितां चतुराननाम् । रक्ताम्बरद्वयोपेतामक्षसूत्रकरां तथा ॥ कमण्डलुधरां देवी हंसवाहनसंस्थिताम् । ब्रह्माणी ब्रह्मदैवत्यां ब्रह्मलोकनिवासिनीम् ॥	Oṃ bālāṃ vidyāṃ tu gāyatrīṃ lohitāṃ caturānanām । Raktāmbaradvayopetāmakṣa sūtrakarāṃ tathā ॥ Kamaṇḍaludharāṃ devī haṃsavāhanasaṃsthitām । Brahmāṇī brahmadaivatyāṃ brahmalokanivāsinīm ॥

Translation
The youthful, glorious and beautiful Devi is an embodiment of the highest wisdom. She is of red color and has four faces. She holds rudraksha beads in one hand and a water pot in the other. Mounted on a swan, She's like Saraswati. She resides and abides in the absolute Brahman and is a consort of Brahma.

14. Chant the preliminary mantra (*Ishta* mantra *japa*)

15. Pray to Mother Earth (*Prithvi* pooja)

Draw a triangle on the floor, right in front of you with water. It's a symbolic triangle. If you are trying to invoke a masculine mantra, the triangle should point upwards (towards the deity) and if you are invoking a feminine mantra, the triangle should point downwards. Put a dot with water right in the middle of the triangle and put a flower in the middle (on top of the dot) and say the following mantra:

Sanskrit (Devanagari)	*Sanskrit (IAST)*	*Translation*
ह्रीं आधारशक्तये नमः	Hrīṃ ādhāraśaktaye namaḥ	My obeisance to the primordial energy that is sustaining the entire creation.

16. Take the vow (*Sankalpa*)

Take it only on the first day of your sadhana.

I ... *(your full name)* born in ... *(state your* gotra. *If you don't know your* gotra, *simply say* Narayana gotra *for everyone is a child of the Divine)* on ... *(state your date of birth)* hereby vow to do a *purushcharana* of ... *(the name of your mantra, like Gayatri, Sri Suktam, Guru Mantra, etc.)* over the next ... *(state the number of days you'll be chanting the mantra over, for example, 40, 90, 100, 300 and so on)* days so I may become a worthy recipient of your grace and attain the desired outcome.

17. Mantra breathing (Mantra *shvasa*)

Start by completely and gently exhaling from both nostrils before you can begin the mantra breathing process below:

With your right thumb, close your right nostril and breathe in deeply from the left. While breathing in, chant Gayatri mantra.

Now, lift the thumb from your right nostril and close your left nostril by placing the index finger of your right hand. Exhale gently. Chant Gayatri mantra while exhaling.

Keep the same hand position and deeply inhale from your right nostril now. Chant the mantra while inhaling from your right nostril.

Now, lift your index finger from the left nostril and put your thumb on the right nostril to close it. Gently exhale from your left nostril and chant your mantra while exhaling.

This is one round of inhalation-exhalation, which involves inhaling from your left, exhaling from your right, inhaling from your right and exhaling from your left.

Do three rounds of mantra breathing.

18. Application (*Viniyoga*)

The word *viniyoga* means application. Unlike *sankalpa*, *viniyoga* is chanted every day throughout your *sadhana*. Use the following mantra with water in your right palm:

Sanskrit (Devanagari)	*Sanskrit (IAST)*
सप्तव्याहृतीनां जमदग्नि- भरद्वाज अत्रि-गौतम-कश्यप- विश्वामित्र-वसिष्ठा ऋषयः ।	Saptavyāhratīnāṃ jamadagni- bharadvāja atri-gautama- kaśyapa-viśvāmitra-vasiṣṭhā ṛṣayaḥ ।
गायत्र्युष्णिगनुष्टुब्बृहती-पंक्तिस् त्रिष्टुब्जगत्यश्छन्ददांसि ।	Gāyatryuṣṇiganuṣṭubbṛhatī-pa ṃktistriṣṭubjagatyaśchandadā ṃsi ।
अग्नि-वायु-सूर्य-बृहस्पति- वरुणेन्द्र-विश्वेदेवा देवताः । सर्वपापक्षयार्थे जपे विनियोगः ।	Agni-vāyu-sūrya-bṛhspati- varuṇendra-viśvedevā devatāḥ । Sarvapāpakṣayārthe jape viniyogaḥ ।

19. Purification of hands (*Kara shuddhi*)

Chant the following mantras and show the appropriate mudras to perform purification of the hands.

Sanskrit (Devanagari)	*Sanskrit (IAST)*	*Handlock (Mudra)*	*Gesture with both hands*
ऐं अंगुष्ठाभ्यां नमः।	Aiṃ aṃguṣṭhābhyāṃ namaḥ।	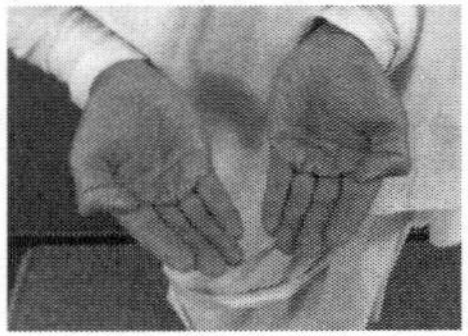	Touch the tip of your thumb at the base of your index finger.
ह्रीं तर्जनीभ्यां नमः।	Hrīṃ tarjanībhyāṃ namaḥ।	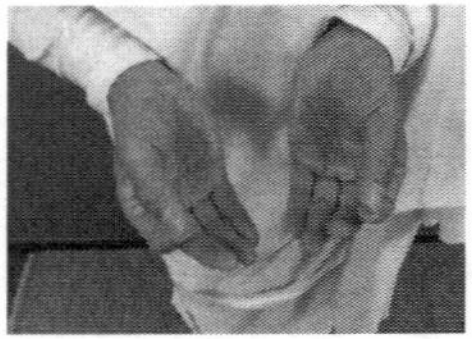	Touch the tip of your thumb to the tip of your index finger.
श्रीं मध्यमाभ्यां नमः।	Srīṃ madhyamābhyāṃ namaḥ।	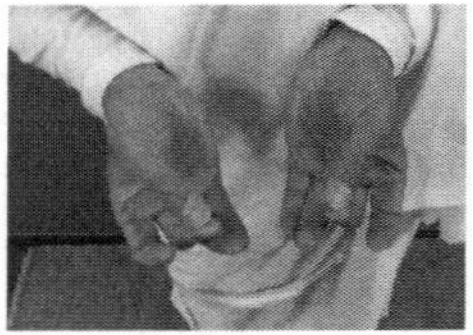	Touch the tip of your thumb to the tip of your middle finger.

Sanskrit (Devanagari)	*Sanskrit (IAST)*	*Handlock (Mudra)*	*Gesture with both hands*
ऐं अनामिकाभ्यां नमः।	Aiṃ anāmikābhyāṃ namaḥ।	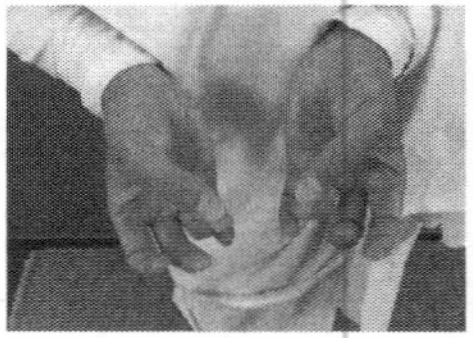	Touch the tip of your thumb to the tip of your ring finger.
ह्रीं कनिष्ठिकाभ्यां नमः।	Hrīṃ kaniṣṭhikābhyāṃ namaḥ।	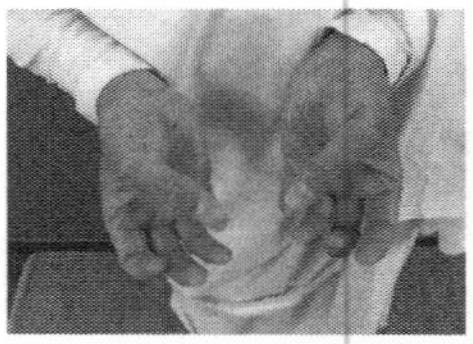	Touch the tip of your thumb to the tip of your little finger.
श्रीं करतलकरपृष्ठाभ्यां नमः।	Srīṃ karatalakara pṛṣṭhābhyāṃ namaḥ।	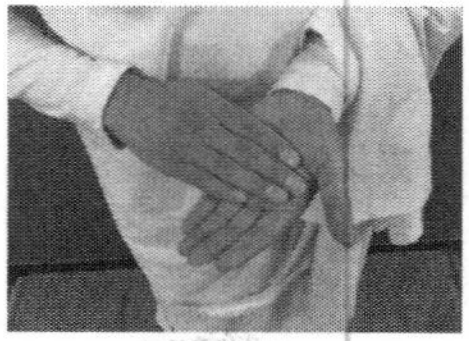	Touch the back of your left hand with the back of your right hand and then clap softly.

20. Unification with the mantra (Mantra *nyasa*)

It is one of the most important steps in *sadhana*. With *nyasa*, you establish the various letters of the mantra in you. You become the deity yourself.

Please do all the *nyasas* shown below:

Nyasa of the sages (*Rishyadi nyasa*)		
Sanskrit (Devanagari)	*Sanskrit (IAST)*	*Touch with your right hand your...*
ॐ गायत्र्या विश्वामित्र ऋषिः नमः शिरसि ।	Oṃ gāyatryā viśvāmitra ṛṣiḥ namaḥ śirasi ।	Head
गायत्रीछन्दसे नमः मुखे ।	Gāyatrīchandase namaḥ mukhe ।	Mouth
सविता देवता नमः हृदये ।	Savitā devatā namaḥ hradaye ।	Heart
जपोपनयने विनियोगः नमः सर्वांगे ।	Japopanayane viniyogaḥ namaḥ sarvāṃge ।	Take the right hand over your head and then bring it back in front of you joining your hands near your heart in the posture of Namaste.
ॐ विश्वामित्र ऋषये नमः शिरसि ।	Oṃ viśvāmitra ṛṣaye namaḥ śirasi ।	Head

Sanskrit (Devanagari)	*Sanskrit (IAST)*	*Touch with your right hand your...*
गायत्रीछन्दसे नमः मुखे।	Gāyatrīchandase namaḥ mukhe ।	Mouth
सवितृदेवतायै नमः हृदये ।	Savitṛdevatāyai namaḥ hradaye ।	Heart
विनियोगाय नमः सर्वांगे।	Viniyogāya namaḥ sarvāṃge ।	Take the right hand over your head and then bring it back in front of you joining your hands near your heart in the posture of Namaste.

Nyasa of the Primal Energy (*Pranava nyasa*)		
Sanskrit (Devanagari)	*Sanskrit (IAST)*	*Touch with your right hand your...*
ॐ ब्रह्म ऋषये नमः शिरसि।	Oṃ brahma ṛṣaye namaḥ śirasi।	Head
गायत्रीछन्द से नमः मुखे।	Gāyatrīchanda se namaḥ mukhe ।	Mouth
ॐ परमात्मादेवतायै नमः हृदि।	Oṃ paramātmādevatāyai namaḥ hradi ।	Heart

Sanskrit (Devanagari)	*Sanskrit (IAST)*	*Touch with your right hand your...*
विनियोगाय नमः सर्वांगे ।	Viniyogāya namaḥ sarvāṃge |	Take the right hand over your head and then bring it back in front of you joining your hands near your heart in the posture of Namaste.

Nyasa of the hands (Kara nyasa)		
Sanskrit (Devanagari)	*Sanskrit (IAST)*	*Gesture with both hands*
ॐ तत्सवितुब्रह्मणे अंगुष्ठाभ्यां नमः ।	Oṃ tatsavitubrahmaṇe aṃguṣṭhābhyāṃ namaḥ |	Touch the tip of your thumb at the base of your index finger.
ॐ वरेण्यं विष्णवे तर्जनीभ्यां नमः ।	Oṃ vareṇyaṃ viṣṇave tarjanībhyāṃ namaḥ |	Touch the tip of your thumb to the tip of your index finger.

Sanskrit (Devanagari)	*Sanskrit (IAST)*	*Gesture with both hands*
ॐ भर्गो देवस्य रुद्राय मध्यमाभ्यां नमः।	Oṃ bhargo devasya rudrāya madhyamābhyāṃ namaḥ ।	Touch the tip of your thumb to the tip of your middle finger.
ॐ धीमहि ईश्वराय अनामिकाभ्यां नमः ।	Oṃ dhīmahi īśvarāya anāmikābhyāṃ namaḥ ।	Touch the tip of your thumb to the tip of your ring finger.
ॐ धियो यो नः सदाशिवाय कनिष्ठिकाभ्यां नमः ।	Oṃ dhiyo yo naḥ sadāśivāya kaniṣṭhikābhyāṃ namaḥ ।	Touch the tip of your thumb to the tip of your little finger.
ॐ प्रचोदयात् सर्वात्मने करतलकरपृष्ठाभ्यां नमः ।	Oṃ pracodayāt sarvātmane karatalakara pṛṣṭhābhyāṃ namaḥ ।	Touch the back of your left hand with the back of your right hand and then clap softly.

Six-Limbed Mantra Nyasa (*Shadanga mantra nyāsa*)			
Sanskrit (Devanagari)	***Sanskrit (IAST)***	***Posture***	***Description***
ॐ तत्सवितुब्रह्मणे हृदयाय नमः ।	Oṃ tatsavitubrahmaṇe hradayāya namaḥ I	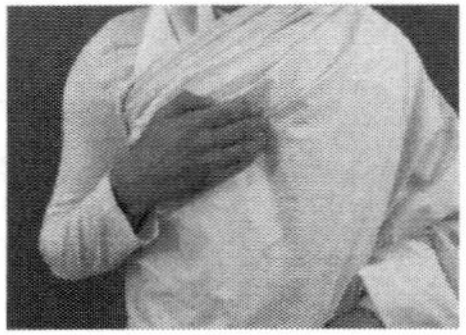	Touch your heart region with your right hand.
ॐ वरेण्यं विष्णवे शिरसे स्वाहा ।	Oṃ vareṇyaṃ viṣṇave śirase svāhā I		Touch your forehead with your right hand keeping the index finger away.
ॐ भर्गो देवस्य रुद्राय शिखायै वषट् ।	Oṃ bhargo devasya rudrāya śikhāyai vaṣaṭ I		Make a fist with the right hand and extend your thumb. Now touch the crown of your head with your thumb.

Sanskrit (Devanagari)	*Sanskrit (IAST)*	*Posture*	*Description*
ॐ धीमहि ईश्वराय कवचाय हुम् ।	Oṃ dhīmahi īśvarāya kavacāya hum ।		Touch your shoulders by crossing your hands. Generally, in Devi pooja, left hand is on top of the right and in Devata pooja, right on top of the left. This is, however, just a guideline and not a rule.
ॐ धियो यो नः सदाशिवाय नेत्रत्रयाय वौषट् ।	Oṃ dhiyo yo naḥ sadāśivāya netratrayāya vauṣaṭ ।		Spread your right hand and touch your right eye with your index finger, forehead with the middle finger and left eye with the ring finger simultaneously. *Netra-traya* means the three eyes.
ॐ प्रचोदयात् सर्वात्मने अस्त्राय फट् ।	Oṃ pracodayāt sarvātmane astrāya phaṭ ।		Take the right hand over your head and then bring it back in front of you to clap softly.

Nyasa of the Verses (*Pada nyasa*)		
Sanskrit (Devanagari)	*Sanskrit (IAST)*	*Touch with your right hand your…*
ॐ तत् नमः शिरसि ।	Oṃ tat namaḥ śirasi I	Head
ॐ सवितुर्नमः भ्रुवोर्मध्ये ।	Oṃ saviturnamaḥ bhruvormadhye I	Between your brows (glabella)
ॐ वरेण्यं नमः नेत्रयोः ।	Oṃ vareṇyaṃ namaḥ netrayoḥ I	Both eyes
ॐ भर्गो नमः मुखे ।	Oṃ bhargo namaḥ mukhe I	Face (Palm touching your nose)
ॐ देवस्य नमः कण्ठे ।	Oṃ devasya namaḥ kaṇṭhe I	Throat
ॐ धीमहि नमः ह्रदये ।	Oṃ dhīmahi namaḥ hradaye I	Heart
ॐ धियो नमः नाभौ ।	Oṃ dhiyo namaḥ nābhau I	Navel
ॐ यो नमः गुह्ये ।	Oṃ yo namaḥ guhye I	Groin
ॐ नः नमः जानुनोः ।	Oṃ naḥ namaḥ jānunoḥ I	Knees

Sanskrit (Devanagari)	*Sanskrit (IAST)*	*Touch with your right hand your...*
ॐ प्रचोदयात् नमः पादयोः ।	Oṃ pracodayāt namaḥ pādayoḥ I	Feet
ॐ आपोज्योति रसो मृतं ब्रह्मभूर्भवः स्वरोमिति शिरसि ।	Oṃ āpojyoti raso mṛtaṃ brahmabhūrbhavaḥ svaromiti śirasi I	Head
ॐ तत्सवितुरवरेण्यम् नमः नाभ्यादिपादांगुलिपर्यन्तम् ।	Oṃ tatsavituravareṇyam namaḥ nābhyādipādāṃguliparyantam I	Roll your hand from your navel to your toes.
ॐ भर्गो देवस्यधीमहि नमः हृदयादिनाभ्यान्तं ।	Oṃ bhargo devasyadhīmahi namaḥ hradayādinābhyāntaṃ I	Roll your hand from your heart to navel.
ॐ धियो यो नः प्रचोदयात् नमः मूर्धादिहृदयान्तम् ।	Oṃ dhiyo yo naḥ pracodayāt namaḥ mūrdhādihradayāntam I	Roll your hand from your head to your heart.

Nyasa of the Letters (*Mantra varna nyasa*)		
Sanskrit (Devanagari)	*Sanskrit (IAST)*	*Touch with your right hand your...*
ॐ भूः नमः ह्रदयेः ।	Oṃ bhūḥ namaḥ hradayeḥ ।	Heart
ॐ भुवः नमः मुखे ।	Oṃ bhuvaḥ namaḥ mukhe ।	Face
ॐ स्वः नमः दक्षांसे ।	Oṃ svaḥ namaḥ dakṣāṃse ।	Right shoulder
ॐ महः नमः वामांसे ।	Oṃ mahaḥ namaḥ vāmāṃse ।	Left shoulder
ॐ जनः नमः दक्षिणपार्श्वे ।	Oṃ janaḥ namaḥ dakṣiṇapārśve ।	Right rib
ॐ तपः नमः वामपार्श्वे ।	Oṃ tapaḥ namaḥ vāmapārśve ।	Left rib
ॐ सत्यं नमः जठरे ।	Oṃ satyaṃ namaḥ jaṭhare ।	Stomach
ॐ तत् नमः पादांगुलिमुलेषु ।	Oṃ tat namaḥ pādāṃgulimuleṣu ।	Feet
ॐ सं नमः गुल्फ्योः ।	Oṃ saṃ namaḥ gulphyoḥ ।	Ankles
ॐ विं नमः जानुनोः	Oṃ viṃ namaḥ jānunoḥ	Knees
ॐ तुं नमः पादमुलयोः ।	Oṃ tuṃ namaḥ pādamulayoḥ ।	Thighs

Sanskrit (Devanagari)	*Sanskrit (IAST)*	*Touch with your right hand your...*
ॐ वं नमः लिंगे ।	Oṃ vaṃ namaḥ liṃge ।	Groin
ॐ रें नमः नाभौ ।	Oṃ reṃ namaḥ nābhau ।	Navel
ॐ णिं नमः हृदये ।	Oṃ ṇiṃ namaḥ hradaye ।	Heart
ॐ यं नमः कण्ठे ।	Oṃ yaṃ namaḥ kaṇṭhe ।	Throat
ॐ भं नमः हस्तागुलिमुलेषु ।	Oṃ bhaṃ namaḥ hastāgulimuleṣu ।	Hands
ॐ ग्रों नमः मणिबंध्योः ।	Oṃ groṃ namaḥ maṇibaṃdhyoḥ ।	Wrists
ॐ दें नमः कूपर्रयोः ।	Oṃ deṃ namaḥ kūparrayoḥ ।	Elbows
ॐ वं नमः बाहूमूलयोः ।	Oṃ vaṃ namaḥ bāhūmūlayoḥ ।	Biceps
ॐ स्यं नमः अस्ये ।	Oṃ syaṃ namaḥ asye ।	Mouth
ॐ धीं नमः नासापुटयोः ।	Oṃ dhīṃ namaḥ nāsāpuṭayoḥ ।	Nostrils
ॐ मं नमः कपोलयोः ।	Oṃ maṃ namaḥ kapolayoḥ ।	Cheeks

Sanskrit (Devanagari)	*Sanskrit (IAST)*	*Touch with your right hand your...*
ॐ हिं नमः नेत्रयोः ।	Oṃ hiṃ namaḥ netrayoḥ ।	Eyes
ॐ धिं नमः कर्णयोः ।	Oṃ dhiṃ namaḥ karṇayoḥ ।	Ears
ॐ यों नमः भ्रूमध्ये ।	Oṃ yoṃ namaḥ bhrūmadhye ।	Glabella
ॐ यों नमः मस्तके ।	Oṃ yoṃ namaḥ mastake ।	Forehead
ॐ नं नमः पश्चिमवक्त्रे ।	Oṃ naṃ namaḥ paścimavaktre ।	Left cheek
ॐ प्रं नमः उत्तरवक्त्रे ।	Oṃ praṃ namaḥ uttaravaktre ।	Upper part of your face (forehead again)
ॐ चों नमः दक्षिणवक्त्रे ।	Oṃ coṃ namaḥ dakṣiṇavaktre ।	Chin
ॐ दं नमः पुर्ववक्त्रे ।	Oṃ daṃ namaḥ purvavaktre ।	Right cheek
ॐ यां नमः मूर्ध्नि ।	Oṃ yāṃ namaḥ mūrdhni ।	Head
ॐ तं् नमः सर्वांगे ।	Oṃ tṃ namaḥ sarvāṃge ।	Roll your right hand over your entire body and clap softly.

21. Preliminary mantra chanting (*Purva* mantra *japa*)

Once you have mentally established yourself as the deity and have completed the process, chant the Gayatri mantra 16 times.

22. Preliminary handlocks (*Purva* mudras)

Mudras are handlocks and they are used to capture the energy of the mantra. Gayatri sadhana has 24 handlocks that are performed before you begin the chanting and 8 that are performed after you are done chanting.

The 24 preliminary handlocks are as follows:

Handlock (Mudra)		*Gesture with both hands*
सुमुखम् (Sumukham)	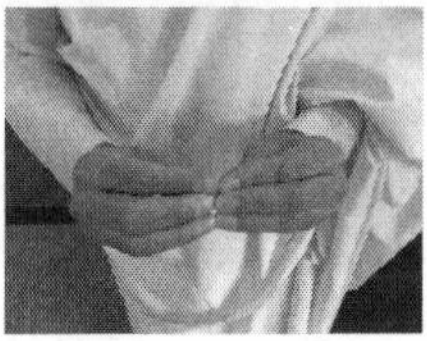	Turn your palm downwards and join all the fingers of both hands.
सम्पुटम् (Sampuṭam)	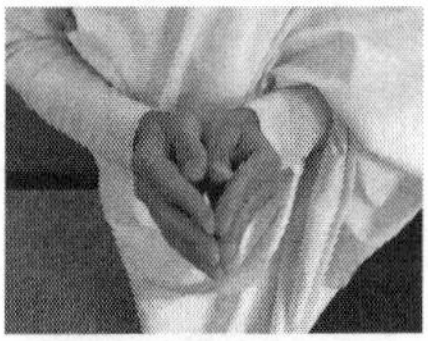	Form a bracket with your palms facing each other.
विततम् (Vitatam)	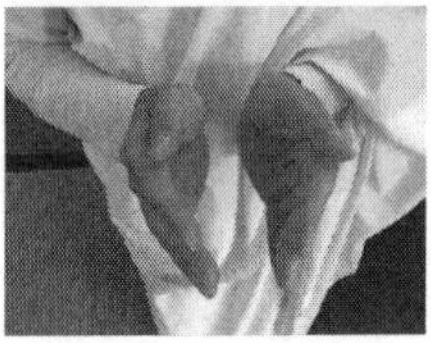	Open your hands and let both palms face each other.

Handlock (Mudra)		*Gesture with both hands*
विस्तृतम् (Vistṛtam)	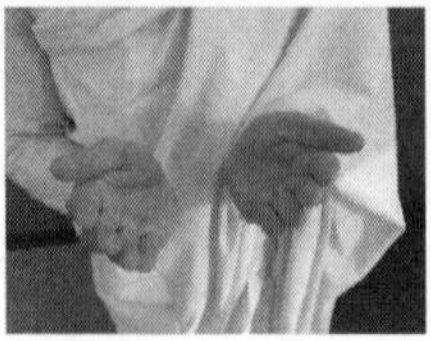	Increase the distance between your palms from the previous mudra and turn them slightly up.
द्विमुखम् (Dvimukham)		Join little and ring fingers of both hands.
त्रिमुखम् (Trimukham)	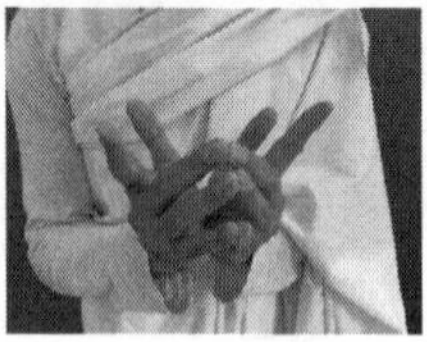	Keeping the earlier mudra intact, join middle fingers as well now.
चतुर्मुखम् (Caturmukham)	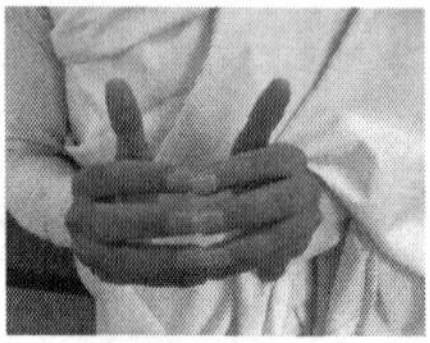	Keeping the previous mudra as it is, join the index fingers as well.
पञ्चमुखम् (Pañcamukham)		Now join the thumbs too.

<table>
<tr><th colspan="2">Handlock (Mudra)</th><th>Gesture with both hands</th></tr>
<tr><td>षण्मुखम्
(Ṣaṇmukham)</td><td>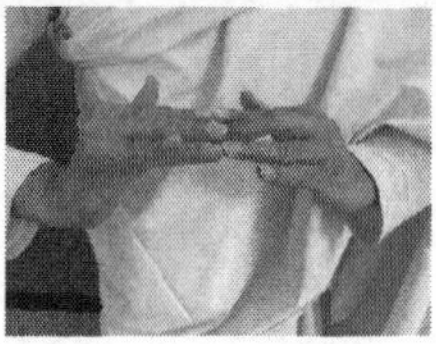</td><td>Keeping your hands joined, now unjoin and spread the thumbs and little fingers.</td></tr>
<tr><td>अधोमुखम्
(adhomukham)</td><td>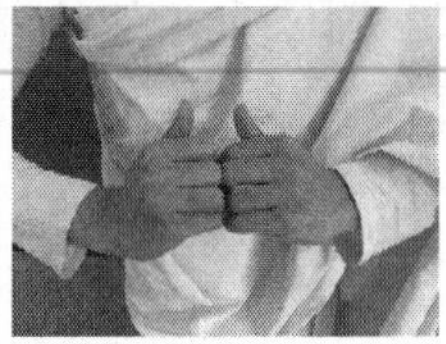</td><td>Bend your fingers and turn your hands over so the back of the right-hand fingers touches the back of left-hand fingers.</td></tr>
<tr><td>व्यापकाञ्जलिकम्
(Vyāpakāñjalikam)</td><td>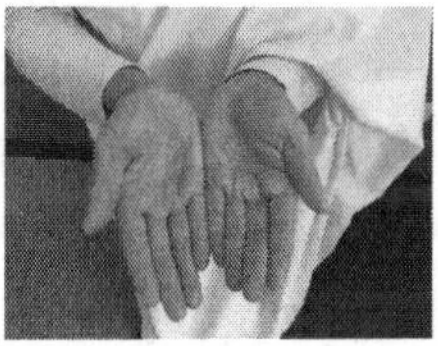</td><td>Turn these hands over and spread so both palms now face upwards with hands together.</td></tr>
<tr><td>शकटम्
(Śakaṭam)</td><td>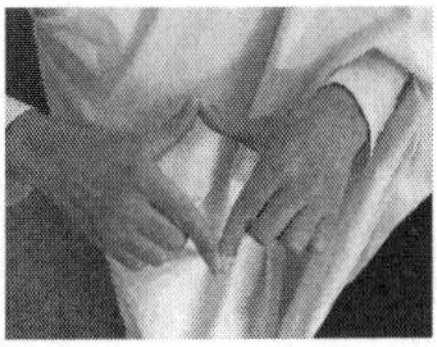</td><td>Turn your hands over (palms facing down) and join the index fingers and thumbs.</td></tr>
</table>

Handlock (Mudra)		*Gesture with both hands*
यमपाशम् (Yamapāśam)	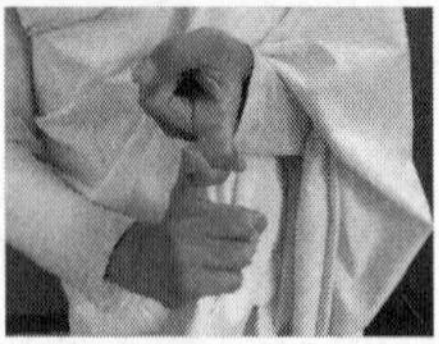	Entwine your index fingers and let the right hand hang.
ग्रथितम् (Grathitam)	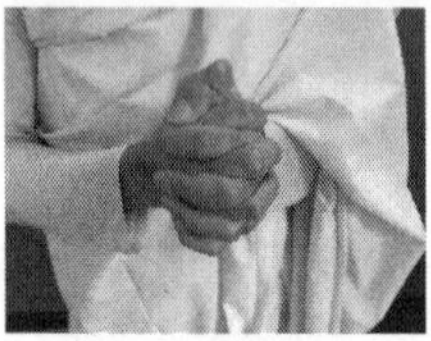	Entwine all your fingers and form one fist.
उन्मुखोन्मुखम् (Unmukhonmukham)	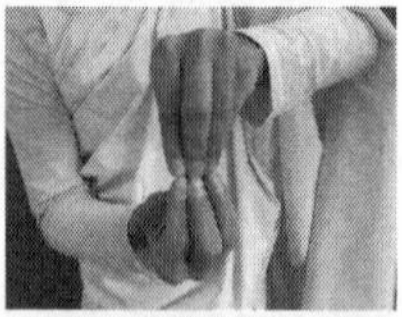 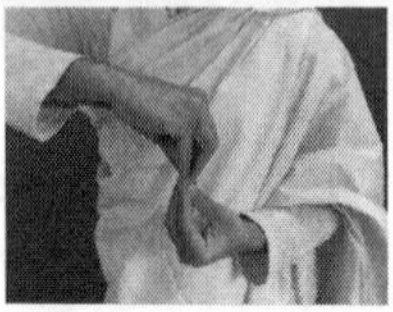	Bring all fingers together of both hands. First, rest your right hand on top of the left and then left on top of the right.
प्रलम्बम् (Pralambam)	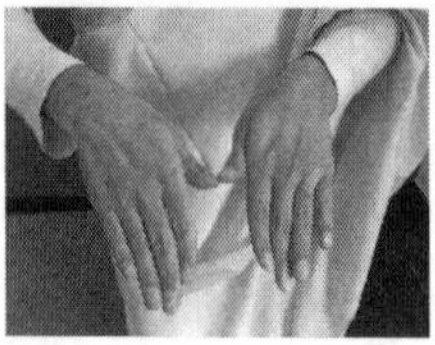	Turn both your hands and let the palms face down. Join gently at the tip of the thumbs.
मुष्टिकम् (Muṣṭikam)	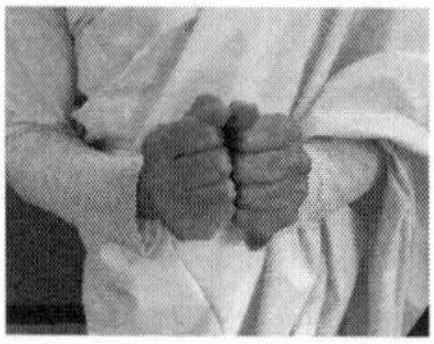	Keep your thumbs out and make fists with both hands.

Handlock (Mudra)		Gesture with both hands
मत्स्यः (Matsyaḥ)	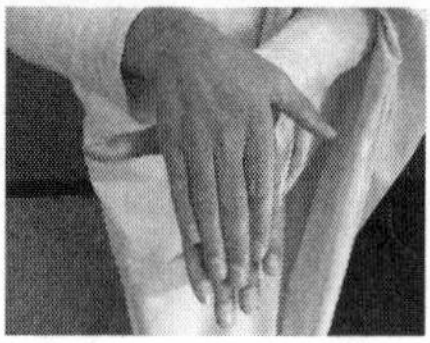	Rest your right hand on your left (palms facing down). Spread your thumbs and twiddle your thumbs a bit.
कूर्मः (Kūrmaḥ)	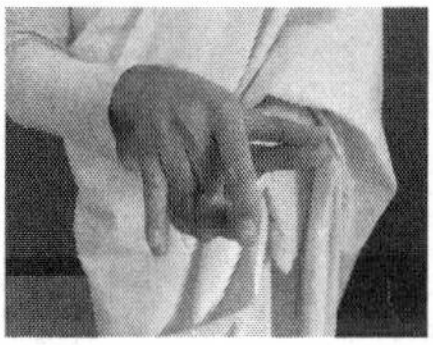	Spread your left hand. Turn the index and middle fingers keeping the other fingers extended. Do the same with your right hand. Now turn your right hand so it's facing down and let it rest on your left with index fingers, thumbs and little fingers touching at the tips. There are

Handlock (Mudra)		*Gesture with both hands*
		other ways of showing this mudra but this is the one I practice and got from my guru.
वराहकम् (Varāhakam)	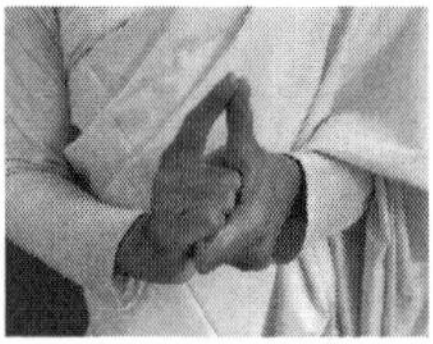	Grab four fingers of your left hand (except your thumb) with right, middle, ring and little fingers. Join the tip of the right index finger with the left thumb.
सिंहाक्रान्तम् (Siṃhākrāntam)		Raise both your hands as in benediction, the back of your palms facing you. (Like in a hands-up posture.)

Handlock (Mudra)		*Gesture with both hands*
महाक्रान्तम् (Mahākrāntam)		Keep the same posture but turn your hands so your palms are facing your ears.
मुद्गरम् (Mudgaram)		Make a fist with your right hand and then rest the right elbow on your left.
पल्लवम् (Pallavam)	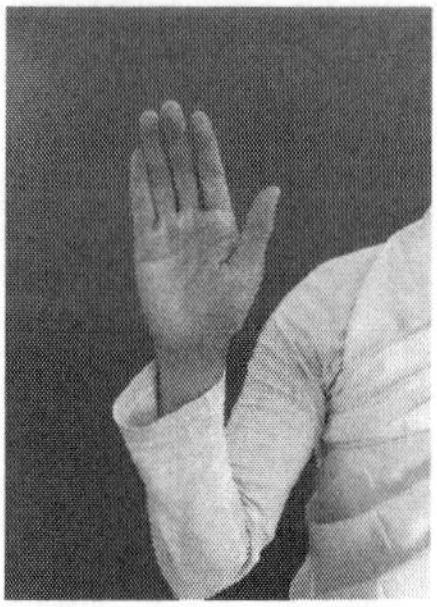	Raise your right hand to your shoulder in benediction.

23. Offerings (*Upchara*)

Make five offerings of incense, lamp, anything edible, betel leaf and betel nut. Say, "*Om samarpyami*" in the end.

24. Invoke the mantra (Mantra *samskara*)

The mantra of Gayatri was cursed by Brahma, Vashishta and Vishvamitra. Therefore, chant the following mantras seven times every day before you do the mantra *japa* to absolve the mantra of the curse of the sages (*shaap vimochana*).

Brahma *Shaap Vimochana*	
Sanskrit (Devanagari)	*Sanskrit (IAST)*
ॐ गायत्रीब्रह्मेत्युपासीत यद्रूपं ब्रह्मविदो विदुः । तां पश्यन्ति धीराःसुमनसा वाचामग्रतः । ॐ वेदान्तनाथाय विद्दहे हिरण्यगर्भाय धीमहि । तन्नो ब्रह्म प्रचोदयात् । ॐ देवी गायत्री त्वं ब्रह्मशापविमुक्ता भव ।	Oṃ gāyatrībrahmetyupāsīta yadrūpaṃ brahmavido viduḥ । Tāṃ paśyanti dhīrāḥsumanasā vācāmagrataḥ । Oṃ vedāntanāthāya viddahe hiraṇyagarbhāya dhīmahi । Tanno brahma pracodayāt । Oṃ devī gāyatrī tvaṃ brahmaśāpavimuktā bhava ।
Vasishta Shaap Vimochana	
ॐ सोहमर्कमयं ज्योतिरात्मज्योतिरहं शिवः । आत्मज्योतिरहं शुक्रः सर्वज्योतिरसोस्म्यहम् । ॐ देवी गायत्री त्वं वसिष्ठशापविमुक्ता भव ।	Oṃ sohamarkamayaṃ jyotirātmajyotirahaṃ śivaḥ । Ātmajyotirahaṃ śukraḥ sarvajyotirasosmyaham । Oṃ devī gāyatrī tvaṃ vasiṣṭhaśāpavimuktā bhava ।

Sanskrit (Devanagari)	*Sanskrit (IAST)*
Vishvamitra Shaap Vimochana	
ॐ गायत्रीं भजाम्यग्निमुखीं विश्वगर्भाः यदुद्भवा देवाश्चिक्ररे विश्वसृष्टिं तां कल्याणीमिष्टकरीं प्रपघे ।	Oṃ gāyatrīṃ bhajāmyagnimukhīṃ viśvagarbhāḥ yadudbhavā devāśckrire viśvasṛṣṭiṃ tāṃ kalyāṇīmiṣṭakarīṃ prapaghe ।
यन्मुखान्निः सृतो खिलवेदगर्भः ।	Yanmukhānniḥ sṛto khilavedagarbhaḥ ।
ओं देवी गायत्री त्वं विश्वामित्रशापद्विमुक्ता भव ।	Oṃ devī gāyatrī tvaṃ viśvāmitraśāpadvimuktā bhava ।
तथा चः सोहमर्कमयं ज्योतिरर्को ज्योतिरहं शिवः ।	Tathā caḥ sohamarkamayaṃ jyotirarko jyotirahaṃ śivaḥ ।
आत्मज्योतिरहं शुक्रः शुक्रज्योतिरसोहमोम् ।	Ātmajyotirahaṃ śukraḥ śukrajyotirasohamom ।
महोविष्णुमहेशेशे दिव्य सिद्धि सरस्वती ।	Mahoviṣṇumaheśeśe divya siddhi sarasvatī ।
अजरे अमरे चैव दिव्ययोनि नमोस्तुते ।।	Ajare amare caiva divyayoni namostute ।।

25. Meditate on your mantra (Mantra *dhyana*)

You are only one step away from starting your mantra chanting now. *Dhyana* is meditating on the deity of the mantra before you begin your *japa*. Personally, I keep it very simple and meditate upon Her using the core mantra. You can do the same.

Sanskrit (Devanagari)	*Sanskrit (IAST)*
ॐ भूर्भुवः स्वः तत्सवितुर्वरेण्यम भर्गो देवस्य धीमहि। धियो यो नः प्रचोदयात॥	Oṃ bhūrbhuvaḥ svaḥ tatsaviturvareṇyama Bhargo devasya dhīmahi । Dhiyo yo naḥ pracodayāta ॥
Translation	
May we abide in the Supreme Energy that is eternal, transcendental, radiant, perfect, divine. May such divine grace always guide us on the path of righteousness.	

26. Mantra chanting (Moola mantra *japa*)

The chanting begins at this step. Now you dip your hand into the bead bag (*gaumukhi*) and start chanting the mantra as per your *sankalpa*.

27. Post *japa* handlocks (*Uttara* mudra)

Once your *japa* is complete, the mudras post the sadhana are shown now. There are eight handlocks (mudras) that are shown at the completion of your *japa*. Rather than showing the standard handlocks as stated in *Essential Steps in the Rites of Invocation (Purushcharana)*, simply show the handlocks below.

Handlock (Mudra)		*Gesture with both hands*
धेनू (*Dhenū*)	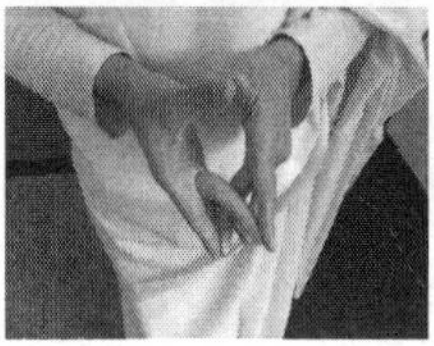	Join the right index finger at the tip of the left middle finger while the left index finger should touch the tip of the right middle finger. The right ring finger should touch the tip of the left little finger while the left ring finger should touch the tip of the right ring finger. Join both the thumbs at their tips. Point it downwards.
ज्ञानम् (*Jñānam*)	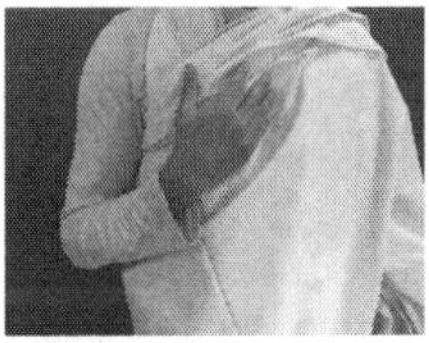	Touch your heart with your right hand. The left is usually in *vairagya* mudra (the one below) while the right touches your heart.
वैराग्य (*Vairāgya*)	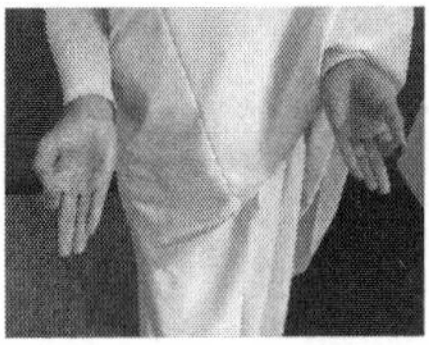	Join the index fingers with the thumbs and spread out the rest.

Handlock (Mudra)		Gesture with both hands
योनि (*Yoni*)	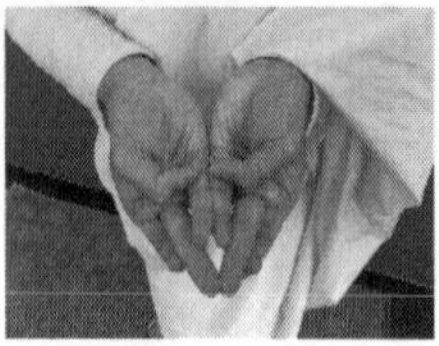	Grab the right ring finger with the left index finger and the right index finger with the left ring finger. Join the two middle fingers at the tip. Let the two little fingers rest on it. Put the tips of your thumbs at the base of the little fingers and you have the auspicious *yoni* mudra.
शंख (*Śaṃkha*)	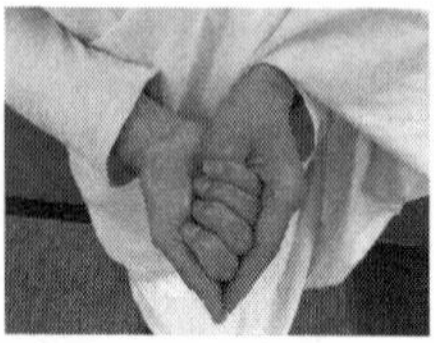	Grab your left thumb with your four fingers of the right hand. Let the four fingers of the left hand cover your right fist with the left index finger joining at the tip with the right thumb.
पन्कजम् (*Pankajam*)	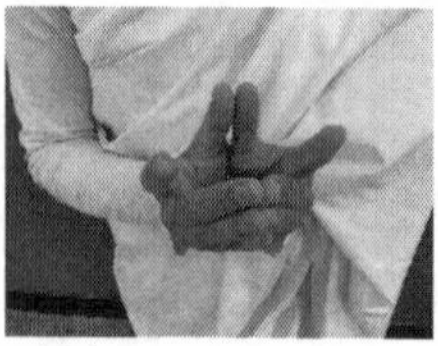	A budding lotus is shown by joining all your fingers but opening the index fingers. You can also spread out all the fingers to show this mudra.

Handlock (Mudra)		*Gesture with both hands*
लिङ्गम् (*Liṅgam*)	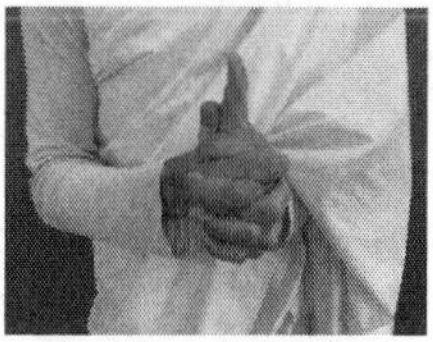	Crisscross the fingers of both hands and stick out the right thumb.
निर्वाणम् (*Nirvāṇam*)		This is also called *samahara* mudra and has been explained in the chapter on mudras.

28. Offer your chanting (*Japa samarpana*)

When your *japa* is complete, it should be offered to the deity of the mantra so its vibrations are released in the universe and it may be used for the welfare of all sentient beings. Offer your prayer in the left hand of Devi with the mantra below:

Sanskrit (Devanagari)	*Sanskrit (IAST)*
अभिष्ट सिद्धिं मे देहि शरणागत वत्सले, भक्त्या समर्पये तुभ्यं जपमेवर्चनम् ॥	Abhiṣṭa siddhiṃ me dehi śaraṇāgata vatsale, bhaktyā samarpaye tubhyaṃ japamevarcanam ॥
Translation	
Please grant me your benediction (the desired outcome) O Devi, refuge of the one who seeks you, your devotee here surrenders and offers all my japa and prayers to you.	

You can chant the following mantra after offering your chanting to reinforce that you pray for the welfare of everyone around you.

Sanskrit (Devanagari)	*Sanskrit (IAST)*
ॐ सर्वे भवन्तु सुखिनः सर्वे सन्तु निरामयाः । सर्वे भद्राणि पश्यन्तु मा कश्चिददुःखभाग्भवेत् । ॐ शान्तिः शान्तिः शान्तिः ॥	Oṃ sarve bhavantu sukhinaḥ sarve santu nirāmayāḥ । Sarve bhadrāṇi paśyantu mā kaścidduḥkhabhāgbhavet । Oṃ śāntiḥ śāntiḥ śāntiḥ ॥
Translation	
May all sentient beings at peace, May no one suffer from illness, May all see what is auspicious, May no one suffer. Om peace, peace, peace.	

29. Free all energies (*Visarjana*)

In this step, thanking the energies of the deity who presented themselves while you propitiated the divine energy and chanted your mantra, we allow those energies to return to their abode. It can be done with any words you so wish to choose or you can chant the simple mantra below:

If praying to the feminine energy (Devi)	
Sanskrit (Devanagari)	*Sanskrit (IAST)*
गच्छ गच्छ परं स्थानं स्वस्थानं परमेश्वरि । पूजाराधनकाले च पुनरागमनाय च ॥ तिष्ठ तिष्ठ परस्थाने स्वस्थाने परमेश्वरि ।	Gaccha gaccha paraṃ sthānaṃ svasthānaṃ parameśvari । Pūjārādhanakāle ca punarāgamanāya ca ॥ Tiṣṭha tiṣṭha parasthāne svasthāne parameśvari ।
यत्र ब्रह्मादयो देवाः सर्वे तिष्ठन्ति मे हृदि ॥	Yatra brahmādayo devāḥ sarve tiṣṭhanti me hṛdi ॥
Translation	
May all energies return to their abode and I humbly request your presence again when I pray to you next. May all energies take their seats in their respective abodes. May the Supreme Energy reside in my heart.	

30. Seek forgiveness (*Kshama prarthana*)

Once again, you can seek forgiveness with any words you wish to use, for, sentiment is more important than language or you can use the verses below to do this.

Sanskrit (Devanagari)	*Sanskrit (IAST)*
अपराधसहस्त्राणि क्रियन्तेऽहर्निशं मया । दासोऽयमिति मां मत्वा क्षमस्व परमेश्र्वरि ॥	Aparādhasahastrāṇi kriyanteSharniśaṃ mayā । Dāsosyamiti māṃ matvā kṣamasva parameśrvari ॥

Sanskrit (Devanagari)	*Sanskrit (IAST)*
आवाहनं न जानामि न जानामि विसर्जनम् । पूजां चैव न जानामि क्षम्यतां परमेश्वरि ॥ मन्त्रहीनं क्रियाहीनं भक्तिहीनं सुरेश्वरि । यत्पूजितं मया देवि परिपूर्ण तदस्तु मे ॥	Āvāhanaṃ na jānāmi na jānāmi visarjanam । Pūjāṃ caiva na jānāmi kṣamyatāṃ parameśrvari ॥ Mantrahīnaṃ kriyāhīnaṃ bhaktihīnaṃ sureśrvari । Yatpūjitaṃ mayā devi paripūrṇa tadastu me ॥
Translation	
O Devi, I must have committed thousands of mistakes and errors in chanting Your names. Please forgive me for my errors like a good master forgives his servant. I don't know how to invite You nor do I know how to see You off. I don't know how to pray to You, please forgive me for my ignorance. I am without the knowledge of mantras, actions or devotion, O Goddess. And yet, I dare to pray to You. Please grant me Your grace.	

31. Fire offerings (*Yajna*)

Fire offerings have been detailed in the next chapter in this appendix. The number of fire offerings should be one-tenth of your mantra chanting.

32. Libations (*Tarpana*)

Tarapana are water offerings or libations, as they are usually called, made to the deity of your mantra. One-tenth of your *yajna* is your libation count. Add "*Om tarpyami*" at the end of Gayatri mantra while chanting.

33. Coronation (*Marjana* or *abhishekam*)

The number of offerings done in *marjana* is one-tenth the number of libations. To do *marjana*, take vessel number two containing water. Joining your thumb and ring finger, dip it in water and sprinkle on your head with the same mudra.

In the end, you can either offer this water to the sun or pour it in the root of any tree. Both are equally effective.

34. Charity (*Sadhak bhojan* or Brahmin *bhojan*)

Sadhak bhojan is usually done not every day of your sadhana but on the last day when you complete your sadhana. The idea is to feed God present in living entities. It is also a moment of celebration to mark the successful completion of your intense routine spread over so many days. In the olden times, an aspirant would either be part of a *gurukul* where there would be other aspirants and feeding them would be enough. Or, an aspirant would gather a certain number of Brahmins. They would come together and with beautiful Vedic chants energize the whole environment. The aspirant would feed them.

Depending on where you live, it may be difficult to do either. So, you can do something else, which is equally effective. Simply set aside whatever you can every day, an amount of money that would buy at least one meal for a person or whatever you can reasonably afford. If you are really pressed financially and can't set aside even Rs. 50 or a dollar a day, then simply set aside a handful of dry fruits every day. At the end of your sadhana, offer them to a fellow aspirant who is also walking the path. If you can't find that, offer it to a Brahmin who serves in a temple or chants Vedic mantras daily. If you can't find that Brahmin, then offer it to any orphanage. If there is no orphanage, you can give it to any old-age home. If you can't find even that, feed it to the birds. If by some rare chance, you can't do that either, then immerse the offerings in a stream, river or the ocean. The idea is that someone other than you or other than your own family should partake of your offerings so whatever you did tangibly also helps someone else.

35. Seek again (*Kshama prarthana*)

Repeat the hymn of forgiveness as in step number 30 for there might have been mistakes in your actions from step 31–34.

36. Offer water to the sun (*Surya arghya*)

Step outside and offer the water to the sun. You should do this by facing the sun. If due to weather conditions or the time of the day you can't see the sun, simply face the direction the sun rises in. Chanting the mantra of your deity, simply raise the vessel of water above your head and pour it in on the ground.

The Arrangement of Pots (*Patrasadana*)

'Patra' means a vessel or a receptacle and 'asadana' means to lay out something. *Patrasadana* is the precise process of laying out various pots or vessels used in your pooja. Together, they are called *pancha patra* – five vessels used for various things and sixth is a saucer-like small plate you use to put aside your offerings. These are usually small pots, each one containing no more than 100 ml of water. In addition to this, a spoon (*achamani*) is used to take water from these pots and to put them in the saucer or your hand depending on the ritual you are performing.

The five pots (*patras*) are:

1. Water for purification (*Achamana*)

This vessel contains the water you use for your consumption throughout the pooja. When performing *achamana*, take a bit of water in your right palm using the spoon. Generally, *achamana* is done for purification and can be different for different sadhanas. For the four sadhanas listed in this book, I've clearly written wherever you need to perform *achamana*. Other than drinking, at the beginning of any pooja, a bit of water is taken from this pot and sprinkled in the air to purify the environment and energies around you.

2. Plain water for offering (*Arghya*)

From this vessel, you offer water to the deity of the mantra and His/Her companion energies. When offering *arghya*, you take a bit of water from the *arghya* pot and put it in the small saucer/plate to collect this water. You can use the same spoon to offer water that you used to offer *achamana* or you can keep a separate spoon for this.

3. Fragrant water for offering (*Sugandhita arghya*)

As part of the 5, 10 or 16 offerings, fragrant water may be offered to the deity. If any particular sadhana requires a special kind of fragrance, I've listed it there. If nothing is specified, you can make the water fragrant by keeping a few petals of a rose in it. Or by mixing it with sandalwood paste. You can also put a drop of any all-natural extract of any fragrant substance like flowers, etc.

4. Water for libations (*Tarpana*)

Water from this pot is used for offering libations to the deity, other energies and ancestors. There are many ways to do libations depending on the nature of the libation and your sadhana, but the simplest way is to chant the mantra for libation, take a bit of water using the spoon (you can use the same spoon as *achamana*) and put it back in the libation pot.

5. Water for washing (*Padyam*)

Every time an aspirant does *achamana* (drink water for purification), he's supposed to wash his hands. This is done using water from this pot, usually using a different spoon and not the same one as for *achamana*. A bit of water is taken in your right hand and the spoon is put back in the pot. Both hands are then rubbed on your left side using this little water for purification. Water from this pot is also used to offer *padyam* to the deity while making 10 or 16 offerings. Take a bit of water from this pot using a spoon and put it in the plate next to you.

The sixth is a saucer. It's a little plate used to collect water. Please see the diagram below to understand the scriptural injunctions on how to lay out these pots in front of you.

Altar/Picture or idol of the deity/Yantra/Lamp

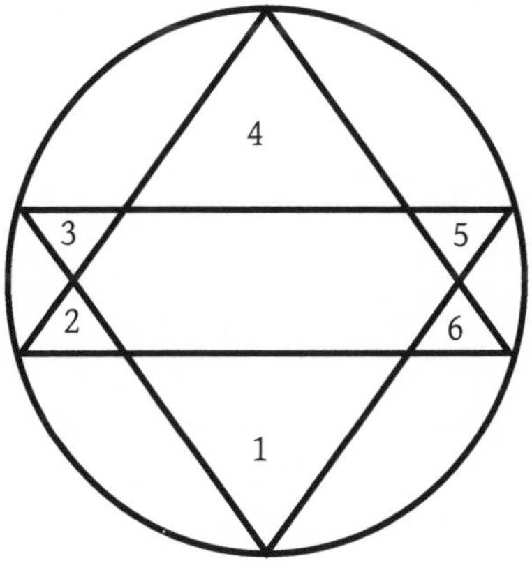

You

How to Make Fire Offerings (*Yajna*)

भूर्भुवःस्वस्तरुस्तारः सविता प्रपितामहः ।
यज्ञो यज्ञपतिर्यज्वा यज्ञाङ्गो यज्ञवाहनः ॥

यज्ञभृद् यज्ञकृद् यज्ञी यज्ञभुग् यज्ञसाधनः ।
यज्ञान्तकृद् यज्ञगुह्यमन्नमन्नाद एव च ॥

Bhūrbhuvaḥsvastarustāraḥ savitā prapitāmahaḥ |
Yajño yajñapatiryajvā yajñāṅgo yajñavāhanaḥ ||

Yajñabhṛd yajñakṛd yajñī yajñabhug yajñasādhanaḥ |
Yajñāntakṛd yajñaguhyamannamannāda eva ca ||

The one who is the essence of the three lokas and three states of mind, nature and existence, that one who lights up our path and is the eternal father, his very nature is yajna. He alone is the enjoyer of all yajnas. He, the lord of yajnas, represents the Vedic injunctions of fire offerings and all limbs of yajnas, he bestows the rewards of such yajna.

He, the ruler of yajnas, is the one performing fire

> *offerings (through me for, he's one without a second, he alone exists). That sole enjoyer and the only recipient of all offerings made in that firepit. He, the final offering, fulfills all yajnas and remains the greatest mystical realization of a yajna. He's all sustenance (food) and the enjoyer of such sustenance.*
>
> (*Vishnu Sahasranamam, 104, 105.* My own translation.)

If there's one thing without which no religious rite is ever performed in *Sanatana Dharma* (commonly known as the Hindu religion), that will be the use of fire. Whether that fire is in the form of a lamp or offerings in a firepit or even libations (*arghyam*) to the greatest fireball, the sun, often the presence of fire marks the beginning and end of life. The fire of passion is the seed of our body, the fire in a mother's womb sustains us, the fire of our desires propels us, the fire in our bellies digests our food, the fire in our bodies ages us and ultimately, it is to fire that we are given at the time of cremation.

Therefore, a *yajna* not only represents fire offerings made in a firepit, but an expression of gratitude towards all things that govern our lives. In *Sanatana Dharma*, there are five types of *yajna*:

1. Offerings to all living beings (*bhuta-yajna*): This involves feeding birds and animals, planting trees, watering plants and mindful usage of natural resources.
2. Charity and mutual respect (*manushya-yajna*): To respectfully receive a guest, to respect other people's

space, existence and freedom, to help others to the best of one's abilities is *manushya-yajna.*

3. Offerings to our ancestors (*pitr-yajna*): This involves donating food, money, clothes and so on in the memory of our ancestors to thank them. After all, even if they left no material legacy for someone, their seed is the reason why we are here.
4. Offerings to gods (*deva-yajna*): By making water and fire offerings, we perform *deva-yajna*. This type of *yajna* along with the one below is our primary focus presently.
5. Offering to the Universe (*brahma-yajna*): This is done by chanting Vedic mantras. Therefore, in mantra yoga no fire offerings are made without associating a mantra with them. For on the path of mantra sadhana, sound (manifest or silence) is our first connection with the divine energy.

That which helps us realize the truth (*jna*) of now, the present moment (*ya*), is *yajna*. Our life is a series of present moments.

The yajna that has fire offerings is also called *homam* or *agnihotra*. It can be as elaborate as easily lasting eight hours or more, or it can be concise enough to be wrapped up within 15-20 minutes. What kind of *yajna* you do depends entirely on the nature and purpose of your sadhana. In this chapter, as far as mantra yoga is concerned, to make effective fire offerings, I present to you the short but sufficient steps of a *yajna*.

Ingredients required for fire offerings

- Bricks and sand if you are making your own elevated platform (*Vedi*).
- An oil lamp. Incense is optional.
- Ghee (or any specific oil as prescribed in the sadhana).
- Any spoon or wooden spoons to make offerings of ghee.
- A small water pot.

  (*Yajna* ingredients are different for various sadhanas. Once again, for the sadhanas listed in this book, I've specified the ingredients.)
- Firewood (Small sticks usually suffice unless you are doing a large *yajna*).
- A dry coconut. This is used in the end to offer the last oblation (*ahuti*). The coconut is punctured (if it's with skin) or cut at the top (if it's without skin) and a bit of ghee and yajna ingredients are put in that (the lid is put back on the top if it's without skin).
- A bucket of water (I've done thousands of *yajnas* in my life and never needed to douse the fire. But, if you are starting out, you may want to keep a bucket of water close by in case of any fire hazard.)

How to make a firepit (Yajna-kunda)

The shape of a firepit can be a square, circle, rhombus, star, triangle, trapezium or undefined. The shape and size of a firepit are determined based on your mantra sadhana. For simplicity purposes and for the sadhanas contained in this book, you need the most commonly used firepit: a square.

You can buy them readymade from the market. They are portable and the most common ones are made from iron. Or you can dig a pit in the ground. Ideally, it should be as deep as wide and long. A firepit of 2 ft x 2 ft x 2 ft or even 1.5 ft x 1.5 ft x 1.5 ft is usually enough. If you can't dig a pit or source a firepit from the market, you can build your own platform, a slightly elevated piece of ground (*vedi*). Here's how to do it:

Firepit without boundary

This is suitable for small *yajnas* with no more than 108 fire offerings of the main (*mula*) mantra. You will need eight bricks to make the most basic one. Lay them horizontally on a clean surface in the following pattern as per the diagram below to make a firepit. Once done, make a thin layer of sand on it and sprinkle water. This is done to protect the surface (as it may have many small organisms) below the platform from the heat that's generated from the fire offerings.

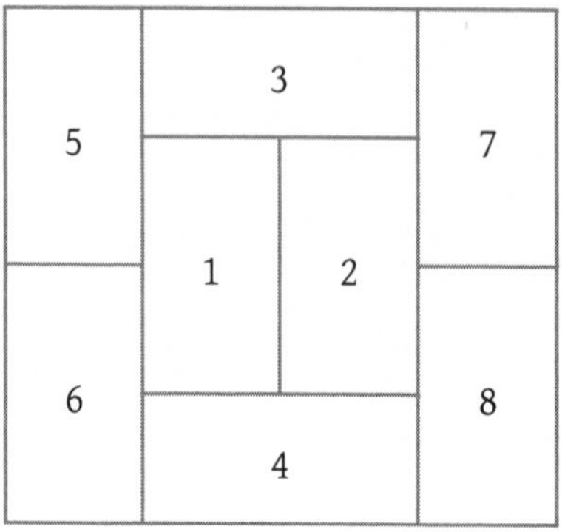

Firepit with boundary

You will need 18 bricks to create this *yajna-kunda*. Make the exact same firepit as in the table above and then create a boundary by laying 10 bricks vertically. This is suitable for up to 1000 fire offerings. As with the pit without the boundary, create a layer of sand and sprinkle water on it. It is important to filter the sand and to ensure that it is clean and that there are no insects in it that may lead to accidental harm to such tiny creatures. You can do this by leaving the sand out in the sun a day before and then washing it, drying it and sieving it.

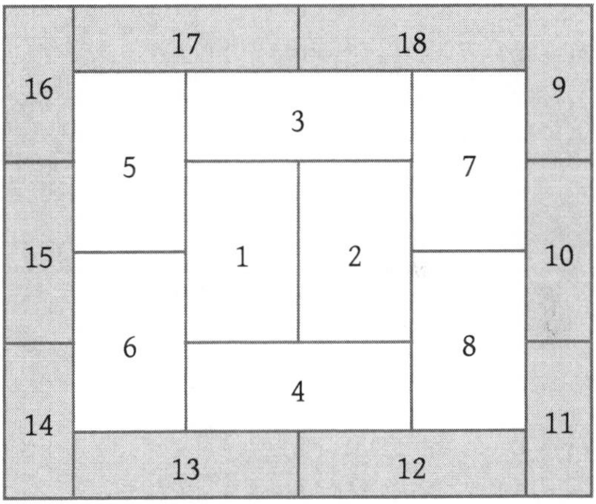

Performing the yajna

Many preliminary steps of a *yajna* are exactly the same as the ones you do before you start your *japa*. I am listing those steps here:

1. Bathe
   If you are performing your *yajna* immediately after your japa, you don't have to take a bath. But, if you did *japa* in the morning but are doing *yajna* in the evening (or vice-versa) for example, you will have to bathe before making fire offerings.
2. Put on fresh clothes
   Once again, if you are doing it immediately after you *japa*, you can wear the same clothes. Otherwise, put on fresh ones.
2. Keep a small pot of water in front of you (or on your right side) for purification.
3. A small container with ghee (clarified butter) will be required. You can use any spoon to make offering in the fire or if you want to do it the traditional way, use a wooden spoon. The two wooden spoons are called *sruka* and *sruva* that are used to make ghee offerings in fire. Keep your pot of ghee to your right.
4. Keep the pot with the ingredients (*charu*) of fire offerings in front of you. Ingredients for *yajna* vary from sadhana to sadhana. For all the sadhanas listed in this book, I've specified the ingredients next to them.
5. Purify the surroundings (*Pavitrikarana*)
6. Self-purification (*Achamana*)
7. Wash your hands (*Hasta prakshalana*)
8. Light the lamp. (In addition, you can also light incense at this stage if you like, but it's optional).
9. Invoke Ganesha
10. Show three handlocks for Ganesha (Ganesh mudra)
11. Chant the Vedic hymn of auspiciousness (*Svastivachana*)

12. Meditate on your guru (Guru *dhyana*)
13. Chant your guru mantra (Guru mantra *japa*)
14. Offer obeisance to all *siddhas*
15. Meditate on your deity (*Ishta dhyana*)
16. Place your firewood in the firepit and light it. You can use the same mantra to light this as you do for lighting a lamp. You can light camphor or a wick dipped in oil to ignite the fire. Simply place it on one of the wooden chips at the base and light it (camphor or wick in oil). Start arranging firewood around it keeping space for the air to flow.
17. Once the fire starts, you are ready to make fire offerings. An important point to remember is that every offering made in the fire must end with the word "*svahaa*". The Sanskrit word *svaha* means to burn completely and it is used to burn all our afflictions. *Svahaa* in the Hindu tradition is the energy aspect of fire. It is responsible for taking the fire offering to its destination. Make the following offerings with ghee alone. Every time, you say "*svahaa*", pour ghee using your spoon (or wooden spoon). All offerings are made with your right hand only.

Sanskrit (Devanagari)	*Sanskrit (IAST)*
ॐ प्रजापतये स्वाहा । इदं प्रजापतये इदन्न मम ।	Oṃ prajāpataye svāhā | Idaṃ prajāpataye idanna mama |
इति मनसा।	Iti manasā|
ॐ इन्द्राय इदमिन्द्राय इदन्न मम ।	Oṃ indrāya idamindrāya idanna mama |

Sanskrit (Devanagari)	*Sanskrit (IAST)*
इत्याधारौ ।।	Ityādhārau ।।
ॐ अग्नये स्वाहा ।	Oṃ agnaye svāhā ।
इदमग्नेय इदन्न मम ।	Idamagneya idanna mama ।
ॐ सोमाय स्वाहा ।	Oṃ somāya svāhā ।
इंदसोमाय इदन्न मम ।	Iṃdasomāya idanna mama ।
इत्याज्यभागौ ।	Ityājyabhāgau ।
ॐ भूः स्वाहा ।	Oṃ bhūḥ svāhā ।
इदमग्नेय इदन्न मम ।	Idamagneya idanna mama ।
ॐ भुवः स्वाहा ।	Oṃ bhuvaḥ svāhā ।
इदं वायवे इदन्न मम ।	Idaṃ vāyave idanna mama ।
ॐ स्वः स्वाहा ।	Oṃ svaḥ svāhā ।
इदं सूर्याय इदन्न मम ।	Odaṃ sūryāya idanna mama ।
एता महाव्याहृतयः ।	Etā mahāvyāhṛtayaḥ ।
ॐ त्वन्नो अग्ने वरुणस्य विद्वान देवस्य हेडो अवयासिसीष्ठाः ।	Oṃ tvanno agne varuṇasya vidvāna devasya heḍo avayāsisīṣṭhāḥ ।
यजिष्ठोविह्नतमः शोशुचानो विश्वादेवाँ सिप्रमुग्ध्यस्मत् स्वाहा ।।	Yajiṣṭhovihnatamaḥ śośucāno viśvādevām̐ sipramugdhyasmat svāhā ।।
इदमग्निवरुणाभ्याम् इदन्न मम ।	Idamagnivaruṇābhyām idanna mama ।
ॐ स त्वन्नो अग्नेवमो भवोती नेदिष्ठो वरुणँ रराणो वीहिमृडीकँ सुहवा न एधि स्वाहा ।	Oṃ sa tvanno agnevamo bhavotī nediṣṭho varuṇam̐ Rarāṇo vīhimṛḍīkam̐ suhavā na edhi svāhā ।

18. Make the following offerings (*ahuti*) with the ingredients (*charu*) of *yajna*. (Not ghee unless the sole ingredient being used in a *yajna* is ghee.) All offerings are always made with your right hand in a *yajna*. The quantity in each offering ideally should be no more than a teaspoon. Hold it between your three fingers and thumb (keeping the index finger away). Any offering in the firepit should be made with a sense of reverence. Your palm should be facing up while making the offering.

Sanskrit (Devanagari)	*Sanskrit (IAST)*
ॐ प्रजापतये स्वाहा ।	oṃ prajāpataye svāhā ।
इदं प्रजापतये इदन्न मम ।	idaṃ prajāpataye idanna mama ।
इति मनसा प्राजापत्यम् ।।	Iti manasā prājāpatyam ।।
ॐ अग्नये स्विष्टकृते ।	Oṃ agnaye sviṣṭakṛte ।
ॐ गणपतये स्वाहा ।	Oṃ gaṇapataye svāhā ।
इदं गणपतये ।	Idaṃ gaṇapataye ।
ॐ ब्रह्म जज्ञानं	Oṃ brahma jajñānaṃ
प्रथमम्पुररस्ताद्विसीमतः	prathamampurarastādvisīmataḥ
स्वाहा ।	svāhā ।
इदं ब्रह्मणे इदन्न मम ।	Idaṃ brahmaṇe idanna mama ।
ॐ विष्णो रराट स्वाहा ।	Oṃ viṣṇo rarāṭa svāhā ।
इदं विष्णवे इदन्न मम ।	Idaṃ viṣṇave idanna mama ।
ॐ नमः शम्भवाय च स्वाहा ।	Oṃ namaḥ śambhavāya ca svāhā ।
इदं शम्भवाय इदन्न म ।।	Idaṃ śambhavāya idanna ma ।।
अधिदेवेभ्य स्वाहा ।	Adhidevebhya svāhā ।

Sanskrit (Devanagari)	*Sanskrit (IAST)*
प्रत्यधिदेवेभ्यः स्वाहा ।	Pratyadhidevebhyaḥ svāhā ।
पंचलोकपालेभ्यः स्वाहा ।	Paṃcalokapālebhyaḥ svāhā ।
दशदिक्पालेभ्यः स्वाहा ।	Daśadikpālebhyaḥ svāhā ।
वरुणदेवाय स्वाहा ।	Varuṇadevāya svāhā ।
वास्तुकाय स्वाहा ।	Vāstukāya svāhā ।
गौर्य्यादिषोडश मातृभ्यः स्वाहा ।	Gauryyādiṣoḍaśa mātṛbhyaḥ svāhā ।
प्रधानदेवाय स्वाहा ।	Pradhānadevāya svāhā ।
सर्वेभ्यो देवेभ्यः स्वाहा ।।	Sarvebhyo devebhyaḥ svāhā ।।

19. Make the five offerings with ghee alone:

Sanskrit (Devanagari)	*Sanskrit (IAST)*
ॐ प्राणाय स्वाहा ।	Oṃ prāṇāya svāhā ।
ॐ अपानाय स्वाहा ।	Oṃ apānāya svāhā ।
ॐ व्यानाय स्वाहा ।	Oṃ vyānāya svāhā ।
ॐ उदानाय स्वाहा ।	Oṃ udānāya svāhā ।
ॐ समानाय स्वाहा ।।	oṃ samānāya svāhā ।।

20. Now you are ready to make offerings with Gayatri mantra. An important practical aspect to mention here is counting. Since, now you are making offerings with your right hand, you may not be able to do the counting with beads. In that case, you have two options to choose from. You can choose whichever you are comfortable with.

a. Use counting beads. You can keep loose beads or pebbles on the side and move a pebble with your left hand every time you make an offering with your right one.
b. Simply see how long it takes you to chant your mantra using a timer. Add 20% time to it to cater for slow chanting at times. For example, let's say you have to make 100 offerings. If it takes you 10 seconds to chant your mantra, it'll take you 1000 seconds to chant it 100 times. Adding 20% will make it 1200 seconds or 20 minutes. When you come to this step, set aside 20 minutes to make fire offerings with your mantra. It is okay to offer a bit more than required so don't be worried if you are overdoing it. The main thing is to not do it less than the minimum number required.

If at any time, you feel the fire is ebbing in the pit, pour more ghee and/or place more firewood. Whenever you pour more ghee, do it with your main mantra and don't forget to add "*Om svaha*" in the end.

21. Now make the following five offerings again with ghee.
22. Make the last offering by placing the dry coconut (filled with *yajna* ingredients and a bit of ghee) in the middle of the firepit. Do this carefully as there can be a fire hazard. Chant the following mantra while you do the final offering (*purna-ahuti*).

Sanskrit (Devanagari)	Sanskrit (IAST)
ॐ पूर्णमदः पूर्णमिदम् पूर्णात् पूर्णमुदच्यते । पूर्णस्य पूर्णमादाय पूर्णमेवावशिष्यते ॥ ॐ शान्तिः शान्तिः शान्तिः ॥	Oṃ pūrṇamadaḥ pūrṇamidam pūrṇāt pūrṇamudacyate | Pūrṇasya pūrṇamādāya pūrṇamevāvaśiṣyate ॥ Oṃ śāntiḥ śāntiḥ śāntiḥ ॥
Translation	
May all sentient beings at peace, May no one suffer from illness, May all see what is auspicious, May no one suffer. Om peace, peace, peace.	

23. Fold your hands and circumambulate the firepit and chant the following mantra while doing so.

Sanskrit (Devanagari)	Sanskrit (IAST)
यानि कानि च पापानि जन्मान्तरकृतानि च । तानि तानि प्रणश्यन्ति प्रदक्षिणा पदे पदे ॥	Yāni kāni ca pāpāni janmāntarakṛtāni ca । Tāni tāni praṇaśyanti pradakṣiṇā pade pade ॥
Translation	
Whatever sins I may have committed in this lifetime or any other, may they be destroyed with each round of circumambulation.	

24. Chant the prayer of forgiveness. (It's the same as the one given in the rites of invocation. It's being given herein for ready reference).

Sanskrit (Devanagari)	*Sanskrit (IAST)*
अपराधसहस्त्राणि क्रियन्तेऽहर्निशं मया । दासोऽयमिति मां मत्वा क्षमस्व परमेश्र्वरि ॥ आवाहनं न जानामि न जानामि विसर्जनम् । पूजां चैव न जानामि क्षम्यतां परमेश्र्वरि ॥ मन्त्रहीनं क्रियाहीनं भक्तिहीनं सुरेश्र्वरि । यत्पूजितं मया देवि परिपूर्ण तदस्तु मे ॥	Aparādhasahastrāṇi kriyantesharniśaṃ mayā । Dāsosyamiti māṃ matvā kṣamasva parameśrvari । Āvāhanaṃ na jānāmi na jānāmi visarjanam । Pūjāṃ caiva na jānāmi kṣamyatāṃ parameśrvari । Mantrahīnaṃ kriyāhīnaṃ bhaktihīnaṃ sureśrvari । Yatpūjitaṃ mayā devi paripūrṇa tadastu me ॥
Translation	
O Devi, I must have committed thousands of mistakes and errors in chanting Your names. Please forgive me for my errors like a good master forgives his servant. I don't know how to invite You nor do I know how to see You off. I don't know how to pray to You, please forgive me for my ignorance. I am without the knowledge of mantras, actions or devotion, O Goddess. And yet, I dare to pray to You. Please grant me Your grace.	

25. Close by praying for everyone's wellbeing. You can use the following mantra to do so:

Sanskrit (Devanagari)	*Sanskrit (IAST)*
ॐ सर्वे भवन्तु सुखिनः	Oṃ sarve bhavantu sukhinaḥ
सर्वे सन्तु निरामयाः ।	Sarve santu nirāmayāḥ ।
सर्वे भद्राणि पश्यन्तु	Sarve bhadrāṇi paśyantu
मा कश्चिदद्दुःखभाग्भवेत् ।	Mā kaścidduḥkhabhāgbhavet ।
ॐ शान्तिः शान्तिः शान्तिः ॥	Oṃ śāntiḥ śāntiḥ śāntiḥ ॥
Translation	
May all sentient beings at peace, May no one suffer from illness, May all see what is auspicious, May no one suffer. Om peace, peace, peace.	

26. Have a hearty meal and sweets with your loved ones, or just by yourself if no one is around to partake.
27. Thank all the divine energies in whatever language you wish.

Made in the USA
Columbia, SC
13 March 2023

13725908R00117